Winning Spiritual Wars

Unleashing the Power of the Soul!

Henry L. Razor

S.H.E. PUBLISHING, LLC

For information contact: info@shepublishingllc.com
www.shepublishingllc.com

Cover design by
Michelle Hudson, and
Michelle Phillips of CHELLD3 3D Visualization and Design

ISBNs:
978-1-953163-10-3 (*She*Edition)
978-1-953163-09-7 (Paperback)
978-1-953163-40-0 (eBook)

First Edition: May 2021

10 9 8 7 6 5 4 3 2 1

Acknowledgements

First, I give thanks to God for His direction and guidance while preparing this work for distribution. When I had questions, He answered them; when I didn't quite get it, He explained it to me. When I needed confirmation, He directed me to the right places at the right times. God, you continue to show yourself great and for this, I am grateful.

To my daughter-in-law, LaRita, who project managed this book from start to finish, you are one in a million and your commitment to success and perfection is unmatched.

I must acknowledge my graphics artists, Michelle Hudson and Michelle Phillips for the cover design. Rev. Raymond Bennett and Johnae Brown, thank you for your thought-provoking illustrations.

Last, but certainly not least, Ms. Kathy Callahan who, after attending one of my Spiritual Warfare conferences, demanded that I put this information and knowledge in book form so that it would become available to the world.

Pastor Henry Lee Razor

Dedication

This book is dedicated to my loving wife, Janette. You have stood with me throughout the good, bad, indifferent, etc. We have enjoyed and continue to enjoy a tremendously blessed life together.

Your support has enabled me to look beyond my failings and pursue the better things in life. I don't know where I would be today had God not placed you in my life and gave you the co-leadership role of spouse, mother, confidant, lover and so many other good and life supporting roles.

One thing I would like you to forever know, is that I do now and will always love you, remain committed to you and do everything that I possibly can to make each successive day of your life more pleasant than the previous day.

Table of Contents

Foreword

It was with great pleasure that I accepted the invitation to provide the foreword for this book. This powerful literary work is both a refreshing and enlightening contribution to the field of Spiritual Warfare. As the Presiding Bishop of Pilgrim Assemblies International, I understand the importance of defeating the spiritual opposition that we, as believers, face daily. Proper instruction, guidance, strategies and techniques are necessary to obtain victory in spiritual battles and are of utter importance. Simply put, believers are at war and must utilize every tool and weapon at our disposal to ensure triumph over the adversary.

I've known Pastor Henry for several years, and he's always been a man of faith, guided by the principles of the scripture. He has been endowed with an abundance of spiritual insight, knowledge and revelation. His practical application of God's word has produced noticeable results in his family, church and community. It is this spiritual insight and practical biblical knowledge that elevates the potency of this book.

In this book, Pastor Henry does an incomparable job of stressing the importance of strategizing prior to facing our spiritual enemy. He insightfully uses scripture to take us back to the Paleolithic period to explain why Satan is our enemy. Pastor Henry then brings us into the Adamic age. He precisely explains how God's original intent was for mankind to defeat spiritual opposition in consideration of the creation of Adam. In doing so, he provides one of the most comprehensive explanations of the tri-part man that is currently available in any space. It is within this explanation that the power of the soul and its function is emphasized and highlighted as it relates to the Spirit realm. With the foundation of spiritual warfare in place, Pastor Henry presents a four-step process for warring and winning spiritual battles. In accordance with the rest of the book, these four steps are also supported by scripture. In addition, these steps are relatable and easy to understand. I'd also describe them as practical and powerful! Pastor Henry closes this book by giving an example of Jesus using this process to defeat Satan.

This book is a must-read, and the application of its principles will yield undeniable benefits for believing readers. Pastor Henry introduces and explains terms like 'Dual Citizenship', 'Spiritual Sponsors' and spiritual 'Best Practice'. He also defines Spiritual Warfare in a manner that empowers and assures believers that they will see victory! This book is a sourcebook for believers and an ever-ready reference for anyone determined to ascertain freedom from the torments of inimical spiritual forces. Readers will finally gain the strength, confidence and skill set to place Satan under their feet!

I highly recommend this book.

Archbishop William Hudson III
Presiding Prelate of Pilgrim Assemblies International

Preface

I wrote this book after years of prayer, fasting and Bible study. After acquiring an understanding of God's desire that I live, be healthy and be successful, I noticed that there was always opposition standing in between me and 'the success that God said was mine. However, I knew that if God had it for me, then it must be mine, so I was determined to learn how to take possession of it.

Taking possession required that I learn as much as I could about my opposition. I learned why this opposition existed, where this opposition resided, what this opposition wanted and what really made me the enemy of this opposition. This forced me to learn how to defeat this opposing force and possess what God said was mine. I had to learn who I am and why I was wonderfully created. Learning who I am, revealed the power that God invested in me to subdue all opposition.

This book verbalizes the knowledge and the technique required to overcome supernatural enemies. Some have, by chance, utilized this technique, but without knowledge and understanding, they didn't or couldn't verbalize it. Simply put, this book verbalizes the process of defeating spiritual forces that oppose your success.

Introduction

Spiritual Warfare has long been a heavily emphasized topic among believers. Understanding that the enemies of God and God's people are not of the natural or physical world, believers have long sought methods and ways to put down and defeat supernatural, or spiritual, enemies.

Careful analysis and Bible study reveals the '*best practice*' technique for waging, then winning wars against enemies that are not of the natural world. Although these wars are winnable, and Christian believers are expected to win, all too often, we encounter defeat simply because of the lack of knowledge about the process.

Winning wars against opposition that is not of the natural material world requires knowledge of the enemy, an understanding of the basis for the fight, knowledge of the power and ability that God has invested in you and confidence in the omnipotent God that guarantees you victory.

This book is the culmination of years of Bible study, prayer, fasting and studying in general. I can remember when God first begin to reveal this information to me. It came in bits and pieces over the course of about six years. I would preach a message, and then realize that the message was connected to a previous message. As I stayed before God, He began to connect these messages for me, and my eyes were opened to numerous things. Truly, my understanding was enlightened. Of course, with everything that God does, He provides biblical support and scriptural reference.

I began disseminating the information and knowledge in this book by conducting 6–7 hour seminars and conferences. Many of the attendees communicated to me how this changed their lives. The information was so well received, that many of the attendees requested a book detailing the information presented during these conferences. Initially, I rejected the idea of a book, but after feeling the leading of the Lord to write, I worked feverishly to put what I believe that God had revealed to me on paper.

This book begins by providing the reason for the fight, as well as what we possess that our enemy is willing to fight to obtain. It then outlines in-depth knowledge on the makeup of man relative to spiritual battles. This leads into a biblically supported, God-inspired four-step 'best practice' technique that, when used, will defeat enemies and opposition that are not of this world.

Finally, this book concludes with an example of Jesus utilizing the best practice put forth in this book to put down his spiritual enemy.

I am sure that you will learn a lot from the pages of this book, because I surely learned much as God inspired me to put this on paper. I believe this book to be a God-inspired revelation of His scriptures that are to be applied when warring against supernatural foes.

I introduce a few not commonly used terms and phrases that I define in the appendix for clarity.

I am sure that if applied, the information provided and the technique explained in detail, will enable you to defeat your enemy in any, all and every battle.

1

Preparing for a War

31. Or what king, going out to encounter another king in war, will not sit down first and deliberate whether he is able with ten thousand to meet him who comes against him with twenty thousand?

32. And if not, while the other is yet a great way off, he sends a delegation and asks for terms of peace.

St. Luke 14:31-32 ESV

BEFORE WE BEGIN LAYING THE GROUNDWORK for spiritual warfare success, a few other things must first, be known and understood. Preparation is required to succeed in everything of importance. Warring in the spirit is no different. Without proper preparation, you are guaranteed to be the spiritual victim, as opposed to the victor. As the old wise saying goes, "If you fail to plan, you are really planning to fail." Let's take the time required to lay the groundwork for successful spiritual warfare and the preparation required.

I opened this chapter by quoting the words spoken by Jesus in St. Luke 14:31-32. I will repeat it here as it is both critical and foundational to the central point of this chapter.

> *31. Or what king, going out to encounter another king in war, will not sit down first and deliberate*

whether he is able with ten thousand to meet him
who comes against him with twenty thousand?
32. And if not, while the other is yet a great way off,
he sends a delegation and asks for terms of peace.

St. Luke 14:31-32 ESV

It is in these two verses that Jesus shares what we have come to know as *'common sense'*. He asks a rhetorical question, specifically to make those listening, think. He then arrives at a conclusion that has a basis in logic and common sense. After this, He supplies the likely outcome if one fails to apply the correct answer to His question. A rhetorical question is a powerful tool when strategically placed in a discourse, with those who question your position on a topic. It causes one to examine himself/herself and ask within, "What does my answer to this question say about me as a person?"

So Jesus' question is a basic one. What king goes to war without first considering what's needed to win? After all, is it not the goal, mission and primary objective of anyone engaging in conflict to come out victorious? If victory is not the ultimate goal, then for what reasons are you fighting? Moreover, if victory is the intended outcome, then isn't obtaining victory important enough to prepare? Oh how foolish it is to engage an enemy without acquiring all of the knowledge possible about that enemy; without learning the enemy's fighting strategy; without learning the history of that enemy in similar engagements against other opposition.

Once this information is obtained about your enemy, you can then create a specific battle plan for the attack and exploit the weaknesses of the enemy that you learned while in preparation. The end result should be victory!

Yet, every day, many engage in warfare with a spiritual enemy without this very basic information, thus greatly minimizing their chance of a victorious outcome. Without this basic preparation, you are at a great disadvantage. The lack of this preparation places you in a position where you are always on the defensive and reacting to what your enemy does to you, but it has been said that in war, "the best defense is a good offense." More so, you better believe that your enemy has studied you, acquired knowledge of your movements and has a battle plan created for one purpose; YOUR DEFEAT! This is why your enemy doesn't hesitate to attack. He never delays an offensive attack. He has studied you and he believes that he knows your weaknesses. It is in these assumed areas of weaknesses that he will viciously attack.

Christians should never await an attack of the enemy. We should live our lives in such a way that our spiritual enemies are placed on the defensive. Our enemies in the spirit should be concerned that we have prepared ourselves to engage them, and we know and understand our ability and power in the battle. They should know that we also understand their limitations and the power available to us to subdue them. Our spiritual enemies should expect that we have equipped ourselves with the appropriate weapons. Your enemy should know that you are well prepared for engagement in spiritual warfare and you have every expectation of winning. A well-prepared Christian is a terror to spiritual enemies!

The second verse in the statement made by Jesus concerning preparation for warfare explicitly provides the outcome of non-preparation. If you don't prepare for war, the best outcome to save fate and life is to surrender. If you don't prepare, it really doesn't matter how big, powerful or strong your enemy is; your unpreparedness will place you at such a great disadvantage, that defeat is imminent. There is no easier way to lose a battle than to not be prepared. Yet, many enter spiritual battles unprepared and without proper knowledge of their enemy, and the end result is more often than not, ugly.

I really need to call your attention specifically to the numbers provided by Jesus in His statement. Jesus said that the king must consider if *"he is able with ten thousand to meet him who comes against him with twenty thousand?"* So the enemy's army outnumbers the soldiers fighting for the king! How then is it possible for less to overpower more? How is it possible for weak to conquer strong? How is it possible for a few to defeat many? It must be possible, or Jesus would not have rhetorically posed this question. Could it be that the opposition only appears to be bigger, stronger and more powerful?

Let's consider Elisha and his servants when confronted with an army that outnumbered them and appeared to be more powerful than they.[i] The king of Syria was angered because God was revealing his battle plans to the prophet, Elisha. He initially thought that he had a spy within his army and he first set out to locate this spy. However, he was informed that there was no spy, but there was a prophet among the Israelites that was being provided with information by God. This prophet was so close to God that God would even reveal to him what the king says in his bedroom. Therefore, as any king would do, he decides to apprehend Elisha, thus putting a stop to his plans being leaked. He decided to send an imposing army to capture and bring Elisha to stand before his throne.

One morning, the prophet, Elisha's servant arose to begin his daily duties. When he looked out and round-about, he noticed that the Syrian army had them surrounded with a great number of soldiers, horses, chariots and weapons. Seeing this, the servant became anxious and panicked. All he could see was impending doom, as the mighty Syrian army positioned themselves for their mission. In panic, he approached Elisha and questioned, "What are we going to do?" but Elisha wasn't panicked; he wasn't fearful, nor was he afraid. As calmly as he could, he said to his servant, "Don't worry, there are more with us than there are with them." The servant couldn't see it. Maybe he didn't believe it, but definitely, he had not prepared for battle like Elisha, so he was ready to send an ambassador, and negotiate 'conditions of peace', as Jesus said. I believe that the next thing that happened changed this servant's life forever. Elisha asked God to open his servant's eyes, and when his eyes came open, he saw what the prophet Elisha was seeing. He saw the power of God in battle! He saw angels of fire and chariots of fire in the mountains all around them. He saw that those that were on his side were mightier, more powerful, and more in number than the Syrian army that was against them. There was no way that Elisha and his servant could be defeated with such a mighty force fighting and working on their behalf.

So even though the enemy appeared to outnumber Elisha and his servant, the reality was that the enemy was quite outnumbered. Spiritual enemies are experts at appearing to be greater than what you can handle. They do this to instill fear in you. A cowardly, fearful soldier is a weak link in any army and will almost-always allow anxiety to place you in jeopardy of being defeated, by even the weakest enemy. It is this anxiety and fear that the enemy will exploit to force you into an error. Peter writes that our adversary is 'like' a roaring lion.[ii] A roaring lion appears more powerful the louder he roars. The closer the lion gets, the louder the roar becomes, but the roar of the lion has never defeated his foe. He uses it to frighten his target, then in fear, his target makes an error and the lion pounces upon him. Many times, the target is tucked away in safety, but the fierceness of the roar intimidates; and thinking it is in danger, the target leaves its sanctuary of safety and attempts to outrun the lion.

So the very first thing to note when creating the plan for your spiritual enemy is that the apparent size of the enemy, to the natural man, has no impact on your ability to defeat him. It is not within the natural man to defeat the enemy anyway. So your preparation should be oblivious to the appearance of power, size or strength displayed by your enemy.

The second thing to note is that your anxiety must be controlled, subdued or altogether eliminated to minimize the chance of your enemy forcing you to commit an error. In the verse referenced earlier from 1 Peter, the advice and counsel was to "be sober". Being sober means being level headed with clear thought. When you are assured of your ability to win, you can engage your enemy with confidence knowing the outcome.

The third and final thing of note is that you must have a plan and adhere to this plan. Remember those that fail to plan are really planning to fail. You can't engage spiritual enemies with a "que sera, sera, whatever will be will be" attitude. You need a comprehensive plan and you must be committed to adhering to this plan. You must commit to seeing it through. This plan must be constructed on the basis of certain biblical facts that are explicitly provided in scripture, along with revelation knowledge extrapolated from scripture through fasting, praying and insight from the Holy Spirit. We opened this chapter quoting Jesus, and I believe that His words are the basis for creating a plan prior to engaging your enemy.

He speaks about consultations. It is probably not a good idea to create your plan without input from knowledgeable personnel in the area for which you are about to fight. Nevertheless, careful consideration must be applied when identifying to whom you will go for consultation. First and foremost, you should consult the Holy Spirit. Any victory realized will only be realized via the empowerment of the Holy Spirit. So, it is without debate that this should be your first and most frequent consultation. Nevertheless, there may be a need to consult with others as well. Be very careful with whom you consult here. I often say that I wouldn't go to someone who went Bankrupt running a business, to get my business financial advice; neither would I go to an alcoholic for advice and counsel on sobriety. These same careful considerations should be taken when identifying to whom you will consult prior to engaging in a spiritual battle. Consult with biblically knowledgeable and spiritually focused individuals that have successfully engaged enemies and come out victorious. Many times, the ones that you consult with will also become a significant part of your fighting army, so the consideration of their time, relative to your specific battle, is critical.

There are four areas included in this book that must be considered when strategically planning for your spiritual enemy, engaging your spiritual enemy and implementing your plan against your spiritual enemy.

The four areas are:

1. Preparing for Spiritual War
2. Identifying Your Enemy
3. Getting to The Battlefield
4. Available Weapons to Fight With

In this book, I will focus on these areas in detail and provide insight, guidance and an abundance of instruction for defeating spiritual enemies at every level. However, prior to explaining these areas, there is much crucial foundational knowledge that must be acquired, understood and believed, before being applied; otherwise, the four areas listed above will be meaningless and useless, as you will continually find yourself inadequate for the spiritual task at hand and unprepared to face the rulers of the darkness spoken of in the Bible. So let's get started with the foundational information that you will need to start claiming victory over spiritual enemies.

2

The Making of Our Enemy

"I beheld Satan as lightning fall from heaven."
St. Luke 10:18 KJV

YOU CAN'T HAVE A WAR IF YOU DON'T HAVE AN enemy. Without opposition, you exist in harmony with your surroundings; therefore, bliss and peace will be the outcome. This is as it should be in a perfect world, but this is obviously not the case with humans. From Bible study, we know that from the very moment God placed man in the Garden of Eden, opposition was there.

I'm going to ask you to thoroughly read this chapter to grasp the knowledge and information put forward in it. Every scripture referenced should be looked up, studied and applied to the layers of information this chapter provides. I have been in the church for almost fifty years and not one time did I have this explained to me, nor did anyone every mention this in any class, conference, seminar or message that I ever attended or listened to; and I have attended many! It has been through much fasting, prayer, Bible study, research, and guidance of the Holy Spirit that I am able now, to put this insight on paper.

As stated earlier, you can't have a war without an enemy, or without opposition. Equally important is the knowledge and understanding of why this enemy is opposing you; this is the very knowledge foundation that is required for winning spiritual wars. However, I have found that in almost every instance, this critical knowledge is not even remotely mentioned in daily Bible discourses.

We know that we have an enemy that's not of the natural world. We also know who this enemy is, as previously stated in 1 Peter 5:8. He is Satan, or The Devil.[iii] Nevertheless, we fail to explain why the Devil is our enemy. Without this explanation, we conclude that the Devil is our enemy because we have committed our lives to Christ, entered into the Kingdom of God and acknowledged Christ as our Lord and Savior, but nothing could be further from the truth than this simplistic explanation.

Once you know the truth of this matter, your improved understanding of what God has given you to defeat enemies that are not of this world will allow you to confidently place these enemies under your feet.

In order to know and understand why the Devil is our enemy, we must go all the way back to the beginning. In doing this, I will refer to a theory that is little known or talked about today in the traditional church. This theory is known as '**The Gap Theory**'.[iv] Although there are some who deny and reject this theory, I believe that there is sufficient biblical support for the basic premise of this theory. The Gap Theory also provides the biblical basis, consistent with scripture, as well as the relevant explanation, for many things that we would otherwise be ignorant of. Furthermore, this theory removes any disparities that science and scientific findings have with the biblical account of creation, the age of the world and other things.

The Gap Theory, in its simplest form, states that there is a time period of as many as billions of years between Genesis chapter 1 verse 1, and verse 2. In other words, there is a **_gap_** in time between those two verses. Let's take a look.

> *1. In the beginning God created the heaven and the earth.*
> *2. And the earth was without form, and void; and darkness was upon the face of the deep. And the Spirit of God moved upon the face of the waters.*
> **Genesis 1:1-2 KJV**

Now let's dissect this with biblical insight. We are going to take some time and bring in numerous Bible verses as we delve into this, so make sure that you have your Bible and maybe even a concordance and dictionary available.

This Bible opens with "In the beginning". Taking this in context with the rest of the verse, it is apparent that the time period being referenced here is the very beginning; **the time at which the omnipotent God created something out of nothing**. It is also stated in this verse that at this point, God "created the heaven and the earth". Period! That's a wrap! The heaven and earth were created and all was good. End of the story. We know all is good because throughout the first chapter of Genesis, everything that God created was "*very good*"[v]. **God even makes this statement in verse 31.**

Subsequently, in the very next verse of Genesis chapter 1, verse 2, we are told that the earth was "without form, and void; and darkness was upon the face of the deep". Wait, in chapter 1 verse 1, we are told that God "*created*". The past tense of the verb 'create' is used, so we know that the work is complete. It is a thing of the past; and because it was '*created*' by God, then it also had to be '*very good*', just as all of His creation is. However, in chapter 1, verse 2, we find the earth in a state that is by no means '*very good*'. It is in a state of ruin. Now how can this be, knowing that God did not create the heaven and the earth in a 'not good' state? He did not create heaven and earth in a state of ruin. Did something happen between Genesis chapter 1 verse 1 and verse 2?

Now let's jump ahead to Genesis chapter 3, verse 1, and it reads:

> "*Now the serpent was more crafty than any other beast of the field that the LORD God had made.*"

In this verse, we see that Lucifer has already fallen, and has taken up residence in the serpent. When did this happen? There is no mention of this in the first two chapters of Genesis. However, we can learn a lot about the time period of Lucifer's fall, relative to Genesis chapter three, by looking at the fall of Lucifer as detailed in other biblical records. For instance, we will look at two Old Testament scriptures that almost every Bible scholar agrees refers to the fall of Lucifer. **Ezekiel 28:13-19 and Isaiah 14: 12-17.**

Let's start with Ezekiel chapter 28, verses 13-19.

> *13.Thou hast been in Eden the garden of God; every precious stone was thy covering, the sardius, topaz, and the diamond, the beryl, the onyx, and the jasper, the sapphire, the emerald, and the carbuncle, and gold: the workmanship of thy tabrets and of thy pipes was prepared in thee in the day that thou wast created.*
> *14. Thou art the anointed cherub that covereth; and I have set thee so: thou wast upon the holy mountain of God; thou hast walked up and down in the midst of the stones of fire.*
> *15. Thou wast perfect in thy ways from the day that thou wast created, till iniquity was found in thee.*
> *16. By the multitude of thy merchandise they have filled the midst of thee with violence, and thou hast*

sinned: therefore I will cast thee as profane out of the mountain of God: and I will destroy thee, O covering cherub, from the midst of the stones of fire. 17. Thine heart was lifted up because of thy beauty, thou hast corrupted thy wisdom by reason of thy brightness: I will cast thee to the ground, I will lay thee before kings, that they may behold thee.
18. Thou hast defiled thy sanctuaries by the multitude of thine iniquities, by the iniquity of thy traffick; therefore will I bring forth a fire from the midst of thee, it shall devour thee, and I will bring thee to ashes upon the earth in the sight of all them that behold thee.
19. All they that know thee among the people shall be astonished at thee: thou shalt be a terror, and never shalt thou be any more.

Ezekiel 28:13-19 KJV

Note in verse 14 and 15, Lucifer is described as a perfect creation until iniquity was found in his heart. It indicates that he *"was upon the holy mountain of God"*. The fact that he had been in the Eden indicates that as Lucifer, he was regionally located on the 'very good' created earth. In verse 18, Lucifer is said to have defiled his sanctuaries after iniquity was found in him. Once again, the very fact that he is assigned oversight of sanctuaries in the realm of the 'very good' earth leads many scholars to believe that God assigned Lucifer oversight of the earth until iniquity was found in him. The idea of angels being assigned territories has biblical support in Daniel chapter 10. In this chapter of Daniel, we see that Gabriel was sent to Daniel, but he was held up by the *"Prince of The Kingdom of Persia"* until Michael the Archangel joined the fight, thus allowing Gabriel to break free and continue to Daniel. This would indicate that there was an evil spirit assigned to the region of Persia. There are other indications in scripture that support hierarchical territorial assignment of angels and spirits.

Also, seriously consider that Lucifer will be punished for his iniquity by being brought 'to ashes upon the earth in the sight of all them that behold thee'. Even his punishment would be his humiliation in the sight of everyone on earth. In addition, it closes by saying that everyone will be astonished at him and he would be a terror, but never again would he regain the glory, honor and prestige that came with being the archangel Lucifer. So, by the time he appeared in Genesis chapter 3, verse 1, he had been brought down, never to be one of God's trusted Archangels again.

Now let's take a look at Isaiah chapter 14 verses 12 – 17. These verses are even more revealing and provide what I believe to be inarguable basis for the Gap Theory.

> *12. How art thou fallen from heaven, O Lucifer, son*
> *of the morning! how art thou cut down to the*
> *ground, which didst weaken the nations!*
> *13. For thou hast said in thine heart, I will ascend*
> *into heaven, I will exalt my throne above the stars*

*of God: I will sit also upon the mount of the
congregation, in the sides of the north:
14. I will ascend above the heights of the clouds; I
will be like the most High.
15. Yet thou shalt be brought down to hell, to the
sides of the pit.
16. They that see thee shall narrowly look upon
thee, and consider thee, saying, Is this the man that
made the earth to tremble, that did shake kingdoms;
17. That made the world as a wilderness, and
destroyed the cities thereof; that opened not the
house of his prisoners?*

Isaiah 14:12-17 KJV

Note here that these verses start with proclaiming the shock
experienced once it is known that Lucifer has fallen. Now
keep in mind that in Genesis chapter 3, verse 1, Lucifer has
already fallen.

These verses provide detail of the iniquity that was found in
Lucifer as referenced in Ezekiel. The iniquity was that he
plotted to overthrow God and take His seat as the 'Most
High'! Lucifer's punishment for his ignorant plot was that
he would be brought down to the Hell. And this was
described as a forceful eviction from heaven in that his
eviction would cause "*the earth to tremble*", "*shake
kingdoms*", make the world "*as a wilderness*" and "*destroy
the cities thereof*".

19

So let's carefully examine what Isaiah says occurred at the falling of Lucifer.

He would cause the earth to tremble. If the earth was created "very good" as previously explained, would not a force so powerful as the fall of a mighty Archangel cause the earth to tremble, and render it 'void and without form'? It is also believed that the earth was a single land mass, but with this powerfully destructive act, broke apart this land mass; and what was once a singular mass of land became separated and submerged underneath water. So in Genesis chapter 1 verses 9 and 10, when God brought the waters together, the continents were brought into existence. Notice how all of the continents appear to fit nicely together like pieces of a puzzle if they could be brought together. (*For more information, research the Pangaea world*)

Isaiah also says that Lucifer's eviction from heaven would shake **kingdoms**. Since this shaking of kingdoms occurs at Lucifer's eviction from heaven, and in Genesis chapter 3, verse 1, he has already been evicted, there must have been kingdoms in existence upon the earth prior to Genesis chapter 3, verse 1, when we the Bible first introduces Satan.

Isaiah further states that Lucifer's eviction from heaven would make the "*world as a wilderness*". A wilderness is defined as 'an uncultivated, uninhabited and inhospitable region'[vi]. Was not the "*without form and void*" earth, as it is described in Genesis chapter 1, verse 2 an uncultivated,

20

uninhabited and inhospitable place? This is a textbook definition of being "*without form and void*"?

Lastly and more telling, is that Isaiah indicates that the eviction of Lucifer from heaven would destroy "*the cities thereof* ". WOW! This is eye opening. Prior to Genesis chapter 3, verse 1, there were cities on the earth. So there had to be civilizations on the earth prior to Genesis chapter 3, verse 1. There were civilizations upon the earth prior to Adam! These cities were destroyed when Lucifer was evicted from heaven. This must have been a forceful and powerful event to have had such an effect on an earth that was created "*very good*". Is this why Jesus indicated that when He saw Satan, previously known as Lucifer, fall from heaven, it was like lightening?[vii]

So there you have it. There is plenty of biblical support for this Gap in time between Genesis chapter 1, verse 1, and verse 2. There are no cities or kingdoms in Genesis chapters 1 or 2, but we know they existed because Isaiah says they were destroyed when Lucifer was evicted from heaven. Moreover, there was no other time that the earth was made a wilderness by the fall of Lucifer. Since Lucifer had been evicted when he confronted Adam and Eve in the Garden, the great flood of Noah could not be what Isaiah was referring to. So it is pretty clear that the earth was inhabited prior to Adam and kingdoms and cities existed that were destroyed when Lucifer was evicted and had his name changed to Satan.

This would place the age of the earth in line with the calculated age that scientists have arrived at. This would also explain the fossils that have been unearthed. Fossils of behemoth creatures we refer to as dinosaurs. However, the one area that causes many church folk to ignore this biblically supported theory is man. That's right man.

If the earth is billions of years old, and there were inhabitants here that built cities and established kingdoms, how is Adam the first[viii] man, as stated in the Bible? Many Christians date the earth by backtracking to Adam. This method produces an earth that is approximately 10,000 years old and dates man back about 10,000 years. This clashes with science that has unearthed fossils that date back hundreds of thousands of years and civilizations dating back equally as far, if not millions and billions of years.

So the relevant question for the Christian is how can Adam be the first man if there were inhabitants of the earth prior to him? The answer to this question is found in the very constitution of man. I will explain this in detail later in this book, but suffice it to say at this time; Adam was the first **"Living Soul"**[ix]. All of the creatures that existed pre-Adam and in the time period between verses 1 and 2 of Genesis chapter 1, were just as stated at the beginning of this sentence. THEY WERE CREATURES! Created beings, much like the animals. They were not human. They may have had some of the physical characteristics of humans, like the monkeys and apes of today, but they were not humans. They could not be classified as human because they did not have **souls**. A soul is required to be human; and since they did not have souls, they were not human. Therefore, they cannot be classified as man; simply put, ADAM WAS THE FIRST LIVING SOUL CREATED BY GOD, THEREFORE HE WAS THE FIRST MAN! There was something different about Adam. When the Psalmist took note of the creation of Adam, he had to ask the question:

> *4. What is man, that thou art mindful of him? and the son of man, that thou visitest him?*
> *5. For thou hast made him a little lower than the angels, and hast crowned him with glory and honour.*
> *6. Thou madest him to have dominion over the works of thy hands; thou hast put all things under his feet:*
>
> **Psalms 8:4-6 KJV**

MAN

CREATURE

Adam was God's first creation that had a soul. He was made differently from the previously created beings. He was made differently from the other creatures created by God when He reorganized the earth in Genesis chapter 1 and 2, when God gave Adam the command to go forth and replenish the earth[x]. The inclusion of a soul in Adam's creation placed him above all other earthly created beings, but beneath the angels, who are not earthly in any way. The very fact that God's initial command to Adam and Eve was to replenish the earth is in itself proof that there were inhabitants on the earth prior to Adam. To replenish means to replace, put back or plenish again, and since Adam and Eve could only reproduce in their likeness, there had to be **human-like** creatures that populated the earth before them!

However, the real jewel for understanding the goals, intents and purpose of our enemy, is the position that God placed Adam in upon his creation. When God created Adam, He issued to him this following command; have "*dominion over the fish of the sea, and over the fowl of the air and over every living thing that moveth upon the earth.*" That's right; dominion over everything on the earth was given to Adam (man). Now if you recall when I introduced and briefly explained the Gap Theory, I mentioned that in Ezekiel 28:13-19, there appeared to be significant indication that Lucifer was, at one time, assigned oversight (*dominion*) of earth. He lost this dominion when his revolt against God was put down. Now, with the re-organization of the earth, God created a living soul (man) and gave him oversight (*dominion*) over all of the earth. Let's make this point and place emphasis on it, as it will be critical later in this book. DOMINION OVER ALL OF THE EARTH MEANS EXACTLY WHAT IS STATED. MAN HAS DOMINION OVER ANY AND EVERYTHING THAT ENTERS INTO THE NATURAL EARTH. So whether they are principalities, powers, rulers of the darkness and spiritual wickedness, if they enter into or onto the earth, man has dominion over them.

Satan, previously Lucifer, has no authority, power or input upon the earth as himself. He can only exercise dominion upon the earth by controlling, influencing or possessing someone who has dominion on the earth; and who is that someone to whom God has given dominion over the earth? Man! That's correct. You and I now have this dominion. So in order to have impact on the earth and be in authority as he was when he was Lucifer, Satan has to have a human to control, influence or possess. He needs a human host to carry out his plan.

However, God created Adam in such a way that he and all subsequent humans could inherently resist the attempts of Satan to control, influence or possess us. (*This will be explained in much detail later in this book.*) It is, therefore, this inherent resistance to the control of Satan that automatically gives us an enemy. Without this inherent resistance to Satan, I am convinced that everyone would have been possessed by Satan at birth as he attempts to re-gain dominion over the earth.

It's as simple as this. God has now given man dominion over the realm of the earth. Satan once had this dominion so he wants it back. The only way for Satan to get this dominion back is to work through those who have been given the dominion by God; and that is you and I. Nonetheless, because of the constitution of man, there is inherent resistance to Satan's attempt to control, influence and possess. So, we have the dominion that Satan wants, and he is willing to fight like hell to get it back. This dominion places every human that was ever born into this world in direct opposition to Satan. We are his enemy, not simply because we live for Christ and are of the Kingdom of God, but because we have the dominion that he once had, and he wants it back.

It's important to realize that **every human** is an enemy of Satan! Period! It's not just the saints. It's not just the Christians. It's not just the believers. It's not just the church goers. Everyone that was, is and will be born is a living soul; therefore, we are all an enemy to him because of the dominion that we acquire at birth.

So there you have it. This is how and why we have an enemy that's not of this world. This is the reason why this spiritual enemy keeps fighting; he wants to re-gain dominion.

To better understand this, you need to know and understand your inherent resistance to Satan's attempt to control you and re-take dominion through you. The understanding of your inherent resistance to Satan requires that you know and understand how God constituted man at creation. We will now take time to explain the creation of man and how that provides inherent resistance to Satan while equipping us with the tools necessary to engage and defeat him, his angels, his ministers, all other spiritual enemies and all supernatural opposition.

3

The Constitution of Man

"...and I pray God your whole spirit and soul and body be preserved blameless unto the coming of our Lord Jesus Christ."

1 Thessalonians 5:23 KJV

AS WE HAVE PREVIOUSLY STATED, MAN IS constituted (made up) a bit differently than any of the other created beings. Being made a little lower than the angels, but with dominion over everything else, we have a unique characteristic that no other created being can lay claim to. We have a soul. This very part of man establishes the fact that we are made in God's image and likeness. Our souls differentiate us from the man-like 'creatures' that populated the earth billions of years ago, as well as the creatures that are in existence today.

It is our unique construction that gives us the right to claim that we are created in God's image and likeness, as well as enables us to engage and defeat spiritual, or supernatural, beings that are not of this world. We must acknowledge, accept, recognize, and understand the worlds that God placed man in upon creation. These worlds exist today and if we are to succeed in spiritual wars, we need to fully understand our relationship to them. I will be using the word 'world' synonymously with the word 'realm' in this discussion.

Before we begin this journey through the details of warring in the spirit, let's establish, acknowledge and accept the fact that there are at least two worlds (realms) within the confines of the earth that we live on. There is both a natural realm and a spiritual realm. Because the goal, objective and purpose of this book is to open your eyes to the power that God has invested in you, throughout this book, I will frequently use the term "Supernatural World" as opposed to "Spiritual World" or "Spiritual Realm" when referring to the invisible spiritual world. I believe that the word 'Supernatural' best describes the beings that reside the Spiritual World; it best describes the powers that are applicable in the Spiritual World, and best describes the power that God placed in us to access this Supernatural World. Also, I will frequently use the term 'Natural World' as opposed to 'Natural Realm' when referring to the material physical world.

- Natural World – The physical material area of activity inhabited by physical man that includes all physical matter and substance over which man has dominion. Throughout this book, this term will be used synonymously with 'Natural Realm'.

- Supernatural World – The area of activity inhabited by immaterial spiritual beings; the realm where the Holy Spirit operates in the **regeneration** of the spirits of men upon acceptance of Christ as savior (*this will be expounded upon later*). Throughout this book, this term will also be used synonymously with the 'Spiritual World', as well as the 'Spiritual Realm'.

We will see later that the very constitution* of man makes us citizens of both the natural and the supernatural worlds. God created us in such a way that we live simultaneously in both of these worlds. Once you accept and acknowledge this, you will clearly see the power God has invested in you. It is then that you will and understand why I chose to refer to the Spiritual World as the '**Supernatural World**'.

We inherently are birthed into this 'dual citizenship'! The Apostle Paul teaches that even though we are housed in material bodies within this natural world, our major battles are within the world that is non-physical; the non-material or in the supernatural world.

"3. For though we walk in the flesh, we do not war after the flesh:" **2 Corinthians 10:3 KJV**

Just as the natural and supernatural worlds exist, there are also bodies created by God to live and thrive in each of these worlds. The Apostle Paul teaches:

"There are also celestial bodies, and bodies terrestrial" **1 Corinthians 15:40 KJV**

This is to say that God has created bodies that reside in the celestial or supernatural, world and God has also created bodies that reside in the terrestrial, or natural world. Since we must live and fight in both the natural and supernatural worlds, God created us in such a way that allows for this. According to 1 Thessalonians chapter 5, verse 23, man consists of body, soul and spirit. It is this unique make up, and the dual citizenship that it provides, that we must examine to fully understand our power to win wars in the Supernatural (Spiritual) World.

The Bible states that man is create in the image and likeness of God.

[27] So God created man in his own image, in the image of God created he him; male and female created he them. **Genesis 1:27 KJV**

There are three distinct persons (Father, Son, Holy Spirit) that together constitute one single God;

⁷ For there are three that bear record in heaven, the Father, the Word, and the Holy Ghost: and these three are one. **1 John 5:7 KJV**

In this we say that God is **triune**, or three distinct persons but one unique God. The word **triune** speaks to the distinctness of the persons of God, yet the *inseparableness* of them.

Man is created in the image and likeness of God. We are not created Gods, but in His image and likeness. Man also is made of three distinct parts. We have a **body**, a **soul**, and a **spirit**. In this we say that man is **tri-parte**; three distinct but *very separable* parts. The body, soul and spirit can and will most certainly be separated at least once, for at death the body separates from the soul and spirit. It is at our physical death that the body goes back to the dust, whereas the soul and spirit head off into eternity.

This tri-parte constitution of man allows man to have the dual citizenship I previously referred to, whereby we live in both the natural and supernatural (spiritual) worlds.

Once we understand dual citizenship in regards to our creation and our very existence, we can use this knowledge to overcome obstacles and defeat enemies in both the

Natural and Supernatural worlds. So I will begin by defining the parts of man and how they place us in both worlds and make us citizens.

In **Genesis 2:7,** we have the details of God's creation of man. We must maintain focus on the very actions of God in this creation process:

"And the LORD God formed man of the dust of the ground, and breathed into his nostrils the breath of life; and man became a living soul."   **Genesis 2:7 KJV**

In this verse, we see that God:
- Made man from the dust of the earth – Body
- Breathed the breath of life into man – Spirit
- Man became a living soul – Soul

With this creation, man became a tri-parte being, consisting of Body, Soul and Spirit. However, equally important is that when man became a living soul, he began living in both the Natural and Supernatural Worlds.

It is with Body, Soul and Spirit that we reside in the Natural and Supernatural (Spiritual) worlds. Once we know the authority that God has given us in both of these worlds, and how we are constituted and empowered to execute that authority, we can live empowered lives that guarantee victory against any and all ungodly enemies that enter into our area of dominion.

So let's examine the three parts of man and understand the role that each part has in empowering us to engage and defeat supernatural enemies.

The Body

The first part of man I'll examine and explain is the body. This is the part of man that has a presence in it and abides **only** in the natural or physical world. This is the entire material or physical structure of a human being -- it is the physical part of a person. As shown earlier, the body comes directly (Adam) and indirectly (childbirth) from the dust; and at death, it will return to the dust.[xi]

Your body is you in the natural or physical world. I cannot over-emphasize this point! Your body is you only in this Natural World! It consists of every body part, every organ, every blood vessel, every cell, etc. that is housed within your physical human frame. It is limited by the set limitations of the physical natural world.

It touches, feels, experiences emotions and gets sick. It is affected by the material surroundings of the natural world and it further affects the material surroundings of the natural world. It is the **you** that everyone sees, talks to and knows in this world, but the body is not the complete you. It is only the **you** of the natural world. The body was not created to enter into or function in the Supernatural or Spiritual world. It must remain and operate in this physical Natural world.

As such, your body must obey the laws of nature.[xii] When nature says your body is tired, it seeks rest. When it becomes sick, it must follow the natural progression to healing and wellness. It requires sleep, food, water, exercise, among other things to keep going. It enjoys material and physical pleasures. It has material likes and material dislikes.

This is the part of man that has dominion on the earth. However, standing alone, the body really is nothing. Alone, it is merely a glob of dirt fashioned in the form of what we understand to be man. For it was the 'breath of life', breathed into man's nostrils by God that animated the body. It quickened it. It gave it this dust of the earth what we now know as life. This process of animation and quickening of the body will be further defined when we examine the role of the spirit. Nevertheless, suffice it to say at the moment, **THE BODY IS YOU IN THE NATURAL WORLD!**

The next part of the tri-parte man I will examine is the **Soul**. The Soul of man is the part that lives in the supernatural or spiritual world. In other words, **your soul is you in the Supernatural world**. Your soul consists of your mind (which includes your conscience), your will and your emotions. Your soul completes the association of man with the dual citizenship that I spoke of earlier in this book. While your body is living in the Natural World, your soul is simultaneously living in the Supernatural world. We saw in Genesis chapter 2 verse 7 that when God breathed the breath of life into the dust that He had fashioned from the ground, man came to life and became a "***living soul***". We can easily see the impact that the 'breath of life' had on the body, because it was immediately animated, and began to be quickened.[xiii]Nonetheless, the impact that the 'breath of life' had on the soul is what is often overlooked or ignored. This

39

verse clearly states that, *"**man became a living soul**"*. So what was the state of the soul before God breathed the 'breath of life' into the nostrils of man? This verse does not say that at this time God created the soul, it only says that the soul became alive. (We will explore the creation of the soul later in this book)

From this one verse, we can clearly see two pertinent points. First, since man became a 'living soul', then the soul of man is as much 'you' as the body is you. This is why I stated earlier that **the body is you in the natural world**, and the **soul is you in the spiritual world**. Second, the soul transitioned into a living state when the breath of life was breathed into man, just as the body did. With this 'breath of life' breathed into the nostrils of man, man began to live in the two worlds; the body began living in the Natural World, whereas the soul in began living in the Supernatural World.

However, since there is no mention in Genesis of the creation of the soul, I am often asked, "Where did the soul come from?" For this question, the answer is really quite easy; the soul of man comes from God. It belongs to God, and desires to return to God. Ezekiel chapter 18 verse 4 states:

"Behold, all souls are mine; as the soul of the father, so also the soul of the son is mine:"

Ezekiel 18:4 KJV

The soul makes all humans universally '**God's Children**'. In addition, since the soul comes from God and belongs to God, it wants to be obedient to God so it can return to God, but it is not inherently the 'dominant you' in the Natural World, so unless you yield to it, it can only suggest, urge or will you toward correct decisions and righteous actions. This fact becomes explicitly clear in the Apostle Paul's account of the struggle that he experienced prior to having a regenerated spirit. In Romans chapter 7 verse 22, Paul writes:

"For I delight in the law of God after the inward man."

Romans 7:22 KJV

The Apostle Paul is saying that his soul, which comes from God, delights in the law of God.

Your soul is your 'inward man'. Note that this verse refers to it as 'man' just like your body is. It is man in the Supernatural World. It is Supernatural man!

Notwithstanding, your Supernatural soul can't exert its presence and power in the Natural World unless the Natural Man yields to it. Remember that Paul is speaking of the struggle he had before he accepted Christ as his savior. So even the unsaved Paul, or Saul as we knew him, had a soul that wanted to please God. Paul writes in Romans chapter 7 verse 25:

"So then with the mind I myself serve the law of God; but with the flesh the law of sin."

Romans 7:25 KJV

Since the '**mind**' is the presence of the soul in the Natural World, Paul is really saying that 'With my soul, I serve the law of God, but with my body, the law of sin' (*remember that the mind was identified as a part of the soul*). Get this! Even the un-regenerated, unsaved, unholy Saul had a soul that desired to serve God, but his body served the law of sin. Moreover, since his body was the dominant him, it performed the actions willed to it by his un-regenerated spirit. Simply stated, Paul sinned even when his soul desired to do what was right, because an un-regenerated spirit controlled his dominant body.

As long as Paul's body did not allow Paul's soul to be the dominant Paul in the natural world, his soul could not force the body to take any actions. It could only want, desire or '*will*' to take action (*remember that the will was identified as a part of the soul*). Paul explained this in Romans chapter 7 verse 18:

"For to will is present with me; but how to perform that which is good I find not."

Romans 7:18 KJV

When a man is in the unsaved state, he has an un-regenerated spirit quickening his body. Therefore, his actions will be

42

those of the body being controlled by this un-regenerated spirit (The un-regenerated spirit will be explained when the spirit of man is covered in the next section). The actions of man with an un-regenerated spirit will be actions that please the body (flesh). This will cause major conflict with the soul, because the soul belongs to God and wants to please God. The soul wills to do the right things, but the un-regenerated spirit drives the body to do what pleases it. This creates a war within the un-regenerated man. Paul further explains this in Romans chapter 7 verses 22 and 23:

22. For I delight in the law of God after the inward man:
23. But I see another law in my members, warring against the law of my mind, and bringing me into captivity to the law of sin which is in my members.

Romans 7:22-23 KJV

So there is an internal war occurring within the un-regenerated man. It is a war of '***conscience***' (*also remember that the conscience was identified as a part of the soul*). This war of conscience will continue until the spirit is regenerated (you accept Christ and become saved), or you physically die. This internal conflict has a tremendous 'emotional' effect upon even the man being driven by an un-regenerated spirit. Paul writes in Romans chapter 7 verse 24:

"O wretched man that I am! Who shall deliver me from the body of this death?"

Romans 7:24 KJV

The toll that this internal conflict takes on man cannot be understated. I have witnessed men lose their mental capabilities under the toll of this emotional stress. I am aware of the fact that many in mental institutions are there because they have physical issues with their brain, or the balancing of chemicals and enzymes relative to brain function. However, I am also keenly aware that many are institutionalized in these institutions because they suffered a mental breakdown under the emotional toll created by this internal conflict of the soul and the un-regenerated spirit-driven body.

There is another way that this war of conscience will cease, but it is not pretty, it's not desirable nor is it recommended. Nevertheless, since I am on the soul, I will briefly mention it. The Apostle Paul writes in First Timothy chapter 4 verse 2:

"Having their conscience seared with a hot iron."
1 Timothy 4:2 KJV

The message to Timothy was that there would come a time when men would be so evil as to constantly and continually ignore the desires and will of their soul, that their soul would simply give up trying to guide them toward righteous actions. He said that these people would have given themselves over to seducing spirits and doctrines of devils. So they consciously make a decision to yield to Satan, and as a result, the Soul ceases to desire, will, guide or warn. As I stated, this cessation of the 'war of conscience' is not pretty, nor is it desirable.

Now you understand that your body makes you a citizen of the natural, physical world, but your soul makes you a citizen of the supernatural, spiritual world. Also, you should always understand and keep in mind what makes up the soul. The soul consists of the **mind** (which includes the **conscience**), the **will** and the **emotions**.

Although the soul abides in the Supernatural, or Spiritual World, <u>the mind of man provides the soul with a presence in the Natural World</u>. So unlike the body, which has access to only the Natural World, the soul, which resides in the Supernatural, or Spiritual World, has access to the Natural World through the mind of man. Similarly, unlike the body, the soul, being created to reside in the Supernatural or Spiritual World, is not limited by the limitations of the Natural World. This makes the soul instrumental in man's experiencing of miracles, defeating of supernatural enemies, and the accomplishments of supernatural feats within the confines of the natural world.

Since the body is you in the natural world, and the soul is you in the supernatural world, the key to experiencing miracles and supernatural feats is to **make your soul the dominant you in this Natural World**! The body is inherently dominant in the Natural World because it is a material natural physical creation. In order for your soul to become the ***dominant you*** in this Natural World, your body has to yield to it and allow it to take the lead in your life. This process begins when you accept Christ as your savior. Remember, dominion in this world was given to the natural man (the body).

You probably have already experienced the Supernatural soul in action without really knowing what was happening. I'll give you an example.

Have you ever been going somewhere and for some reason you got a hunch or an inclination to go a different way? And after going the different way, you learn that if you had gone the way you initially intended to go, you would have ended up in the middle of some dangerous terrible situation? What really happened there is that your soul guided you in another direction to steer you clear of the danger that it saw in the Supernatural World, but that your body was totally unaware of.

Let me explain it this way in hope of adding clarity to what I am trying to say. When you walk down the street, this is a typical depiction of what you see with your eyes, therefore it is what 'you' the body sees. It's just a typical walk down the street at lunchtime.

But this is what 'you' the soul sees.

So while your body is walking down the street looking and fully aware of your surroundings, it has limited vision in that it can only see in the natural.

However, since your soul resides in the supernatural world, its vision is not limited by the limitations of the natural. Without these limitations, it sees the spirits that are out there.

Let's say that your soul sees a spirit of mass murder in someone that's entering into that local pizzeria. It will immediately begin to give you urges and suggestions to go elsewhere for lunch. After you go elsewhere and return to your desk, you see a Breaking News announcement that there was a mass shooting at that pizzeria you intended to eat lunch at, and it occurred at the time you would have been there; but because you went elsewhere for lunch, you were taken out of harm's way. Where did you receive this hunch or urge to go elsewhere for lunch? YOU RECEIVED IT IN YOUR **MIND**! Remember, the mind is the presence of the soul in the natural world. This type of occurrence has happened to me countless times.

Notwithstanding, it didn't always work like that for me. Before I had this understanding of what was occurring, there were many times when I would get a hunch or urge, but continue with my initial plans; and so many times, I ended up in a mess! I then understood what my elders meant when they would say, "**I should have followed my right mind**".

Your soul is not limited by the limitations of the natural. It doesn't need physical transportation to take you somewhere. You can be sitting in a conference room in Chicago, while your soul, through your mind, has taken you to Disney World in Florida. There could be people talking to you, a presentation being shown, things happening all around you, but you are unaware of this because even though your body is in that conference room, you are in Florida. You will know nothing of the happenings in that conference room while your mind has you in Florida. In the past; we have called it day dreaming, but in reality it is the power of the soul entering into the natural world through the mind. This demonstrates the power of the supernatural soul in the natural world. Every Christian should understand this, because with this understanding, victory in life becomes imminent.

Can you image going into the doctor's office and getting a terrible diagnosis? Let's say that your body hears cancer, and immediately begins to consider the natural processes that are available to it. Nevertheless, your soul hears the same diagnosis, but without the limitations of the natural physical world, your soul simply says, "I am healed, this cancer can't remain, and I am going to live and not die." And if your soul is the dominant you, then the outcome will be exactly as the soul says, because, Proverbs chapter 23 verse 7 says:

For as he thinketh in his heart, so is he

Proverbs 23:7 KJV

Let me take a moment here and briefly explain the word 'heart' as utilized in the Bible. When the Bible says 'heart' it is referring to the spirit and soul in combination. So when that soul is combined with a regenerated spirit, you have a 'clean heart'. And as a man thinks in his clean heart, so is he. So regardless of what the doctor says, if your soul says the cancer has to go, then the cancer has to go!

The key to experiencing this level of victorious living is to have a dominant soul combined with a re-generated spirit. This takes us to the third part of man, the spirit.

Nevertheless, before I move to the spirit, let me provide just a few more pieces of foundational proof of the power God has invested in us by giving us a soul.

I grew up in a church where the saints would start prayer with hymns like "My Soul Loves Jesus" or "My Soul Says Yes". Then they would sing songs like "He's A Wonder In My Soul" or "My Soul Does Magnify The Lord", or My Souls Loves Jesus Bless His Name". I remember noticing that almost all of the songs and prayers had the 'soul' as the main person taking the action. I now understand that with these hymns, songs and prayers, they were affirming their soul to be dominant. I don't believe that they really understood what they were doing, or if they could even verbalize it. I know I never heard an explanation for this, but their affirmation of the soul produced powerful results. I became accustomed to seeing sick people healed even after there was no medical cure for their sickness. It was not unusual for money to show up just when an important bill had to be paid or doors miraculously opened when it appeared as if doom was imminent.

I can remember in the mid-1970s, one of the church missionaries became sick. She was probably about 45-50 years old at the time. After numerous weeks at home expecting to get better, her sister-in-law drove her to the doctor, saw the test results and heard her diagnosis. After multiple tests, she was told that she had inoperable cancer, but she refused to accept this and decided that she was finished with doctors. So she never again went back to the doctor. I was only a young child of about 13 years of age, but I remember her being very sick. She eventually got well and I remember throughout my high school years hearing her prayer, "My Soul Say Yes". She never ever appeared to be sick again. When she was approaching 80 years of age, my sister called me and told me that she was sick, but would not go to the doctor. Her pastor stepped in and demanded that she see a doctor. She hadn't been to a doctor in almost 40 years. After her pastor demanded that she see the doctor, she made an appointment. The doctor was amazed that she even walked into his office. He called an ambulance and immediately admitted her to the hospital. He said that she had cancer and that it had totally obliterated her insides. According to him, all indications were that this caner had been in her for a while, but look at this. She was diagnosed with this some 40 years prior, but her dominant soul stepped outside of the natural and supernaturally kept her alive and well. I remember her being well, taking vacations, loving ice cream and moving and working around the church and her job just a good, or better than many that were younger than her. She was one of the sweetest people that I have ever encountered. Seeing the power of the dominant soul in her validates the very reason why throughout this book, I refer to the world that the soul lives in as the 'Supernatural' world, as opposed to merely referring to it as the 'Spiritual' world. You need to understand the power that your soul gives you in this world.

I can recall another lady testifying how once she was crossing the highway and didn't see a truck coming. She turned and the driver hit the brakes as hard as he could, but all she remembered was that immediately she was on the other side of the street. This is the power of the 'Supernatural' soul!

I could write about numerous such stories. As I have said, I became accustomed to unusual occurrences, miraculous feats of salvation and life's provisions that could not be explained within the natural process of life.

I knew these saints were on to something powerful, but it was not until recently that I understood it enough to explain it.

It is the power of a **Dominant Soul!**

I hope that by now, you realize that the avenue that God has provided for man to exhort authority over supernatural spirits within the confines of this physical world is, that at Adam's creation or our birth, God equipped us with a soul that lives in the Supernatural World, and a Spirit that drives this soul within the Supernatural World.

It is with this **spirit-driven soul** that man can exhort dominion, even over supernatural beings.

However, the spirit must be **regenerated!**

NOTE: I will include in the appendix of this book three widely held views on when God creates our souls. **Please note that the Bible does not provide any detail on the creation of the soul; we are only told that the soul comes from and belongs to God.**

However, there are three widely held views on this, and even though only two of these views have any biblical support, I will include all three because I believe that this is pertinent and relevant knowledge to possess.

The Spirit

The third part of tri-parte man that I will explain is the 'Spirit'. The spirit of man is the animating, vital or life-giving principle held to give life to organisms. It drives (gives life to) the body in the Natural World and the soul in the Supernatural World.

When God breathed the 'breath of life' into Adam, it quickened (*gave life to*) his physical body; it was at this point that the dust of the earth became animated (*came to life*). Hence, this 'Breath of Life' is the spirit that drives man, and when I say man, I mean both body and soul.

The Spirit is also the sphere of activity where the Holy Spirit operates in regeneration!

The Spirit part of man plays a very critical and important role in fighting and winning spiritual wars.

When previously describing the soul, many times I used the term 'un-regenerated spirit driven soul'. The un-regenerated spirit is the spirit that everyone has at birth. It adheres to the natural processes of life and drives the body to act in ways that are naturally pleasing to it. Since Satan can externally influence the desired pleasures of the body, this un-regenerated spirit will many times drive the body into disobedience to God. However, remember that the spirit drives both the body and the soul, so in driving the body into disobedience to fulfill its pleasures, it also drives the reluctant soul.

The answer to the problem of an un-regenerated spirit driving the soul is regeneration of the spirit. You see, Adam's sin messed up God's order, so in order to exercise dominion over spirit beings, the spirit part of man has to be regenerated or re-made. In John chapter 3 verse 5, Jesus says:

*"Verily, verily, I say unto thee, Except a man be born of water and of the **Spirit**, he cannot enter into the kingdom of God."*

John 3:5 KJV

If we briefly look back to earlier when we introduced the 'tri-parte' man in this course, we defined the spirit as *"the sphere of activity where the Holy Spirit operates in regeneration"*.

Being born of the water addresses natural birth, as the final thing that occurs prior to natural child birth- is that the female's "water breaks". That's when she knows the baby is on the way; but Jesus indicates that a second birth is necessary. A man has to be born of the spirit! This occurs at the time Christ is acknowledged and accepted as your Lord and Savior. When Christ is accepted, the spirit is re-made, re-created, re-born or regenerated!

Second Corinthians chapter 5 verse 17 says:

"Therefore, if any man be in Christ, he is a new creature: old things are passed away; behold, all things are become new."

2 Corinthians 5:17 KJV

It is the spirit of man that is re-made or regenerated when we become Christ-like believers. Titus chapter 3 verse 5 says:

"Not by works of righteousness which we have done, but according to his mercy he saved us, by the washing of regeneration, and renewing of the Holy Ghost;"

Titus 3:5 KJV

It is critical to understand that this regenerated spirit equips and enables man to confront, engage, fight and defeat opposition and enemies that are not of the physical world. It accomplishes this by driving the '*soul of man*' in the supernatural world.

The Holy Spirit (*God*) re-makes our spirit when we accept Christ as our savior. When this occurs, we have a regenerated Godly spirit driving both our body and our soul. It is with this regenerated spirit, and ONLY this regenerated spirit, that our souls are able to successfully fight principalities, powers, rulers of the darkness of this world and spiritual wickedness in high places.

However, being equipped for war in the supernatural world and being ready for war in the supernatural world are two vastly different things. In order to be ready for war you need to know how to effectively use the fighting equipment that you have been given for war.

So in concluding the three parts of man, you must keep in mind that the very constitution of man gives us citizenship in two worlds. We are citizens of the Natural World with our bodies, as well as the Supernatural World with our souls.

POINT TO NOTE!

Your body is <u>YOU</u> in the natural physical world,
whereas
Your soul is <u>YOU</u> in the supernatural spiritual world.

NOTE:

The spirit of tri-parte man becomes new upon acceptance of Christ as Lord and Savior. This would further indicate that it was the spirit of tri-parte man that was corrupted by Adam in the Garden, and thus it has to be re-made.

The ___ Breath of God ___ (spirit) gives me to both the material body and also the immaterial soul.

Man

Lifeless body

Lifeless soul

Breath of God

4

The Spiritual War

"For we wrestle not against flesh and blood, but against principalities, against powers, against the rulers of the darkness of this world, against spiritual wickedness in high places."

Ephesians 6:12 KJV

THIS IS WHERE WE PUT THE INFORMATION AND
knowledge presented in the previous pages of this book to
use. Knowledge is of no use if you don't apply it to obtain
the desired results. After all, the purpose of this book is to

share the knowledge necessary for victory over supernatural forces in the Supernatural World.

I will now present the four (4) components of warfare as a *'best practice'* for engaging, warring against and ultimately realizing victory over enemies that reside in the Supernatural World. Every person that is contending for the faith must be knowledgeable enough to apply these steps to successfully wage war against supernatural opposition and enemies. This is the essence of Spiritual Warfare.

After introducing these steps with explanation and biblical support, I will provide an example of Jesus implementing these steps to achieve victory when confronted by His spiritual enemy. These steps are critical, but God created man in such a way that the power to defeat principalities, powers, rulers of the darkness, spiritual wickedness in high places, etc. is indwelling in us by our very make-up!

So let's learn the steps necessary to successfully wage war in the Supernatural (Spirit) World. These steps are as follows:

The 4-Step

Best Practice

For Winning Spiritual Wars

1. Prepare Yourself for The Fight
2. Identify the Enemy That Opposes You
3. Get to the Battlefield to Engage Your Enemy
4. Use the Weapons God Has Provided for Fighting Supernatural Enemies

Step One – Prepare Yourself for the Fight

The Chinese General and military strategist Sun Tzu once said, "If your enemy is secure at all points, be prepared for him." Preparation is the key to gain the advantage, and ultimately defeating even the best prepared enemy. I opened this book with one of Jesus' quotes on preparation for war.[xiv] **It has been stated that if you fail to plan, then what you are really doing is planning to fail. You will never defeat a determined enemy without proper planning and preparation.**

As previously explained, our enemy is our enemy because we have the dominion that he wants. He believes it is his because it was taken from him and he wants it back.[xv] So he initiated a war against all mankind from the very beginning, and Bible study indicates that he will continue this fight until he is placed in eternal punishment by God.[xvi]

With such an enemy, it is imperative that we always remain prepared for an attack; we must live prepared, we must sleep prepared, we must wake up prepared. Every moment of our existence should find us prepared to defend the dominion that we have been given and put down any opposition that attempts to subdue us. We must prepare as if we are always in the cross hairs of the enemy and an attack is imminent. Jesus said in Matthew chapter 24 verse 43:

"But know this, that if the goodman of the house had known in what watch the thief would come, he would have watched, and would not have suffered his house to be broken up."

Matthew 24:43 KJV

When we know the details of our enemy's attack on us, we can prepare and spare our families and ourselves the pain of being defeated simply because we are not prepared. The cost of being unprepared is, in itself, a tremendous price to pay! In addition, there is no better advice, counsel or guidance for spiritual warfare preparation than the guidance that the Apostle Paul gives to the church at Ephesus. Ephesians chapter 6 verses 13 through 18 states:

"13. Wherefore take unto you the whole armour of God, that ye may be able to withstand in the evil day, and having done all, to stand.
14. Stand therefore, having your loins girt about with truth, and having on the breastplate of righteousness;
15. And your feet shod with the preparation of the gospel of peace;
16. Above all, taking the shield of faith, wherewith ye shall be able to quench all the fiery darts of the wicked.
17. And take the helmet of salvation, and the sword of the Spirit, which is the word of God:
18. Praying always with all prayer and supplication in the Spirit, and watching thereunto with all perseverance and supplication for all saints;"

We will cover every piece of protective equipment, every spiritual weapon and each applicable technique listed in Ephesians 6:13-18. **Nevertheless, it is important to note that these verses only provide guidance on preparation.** They do not instruct or teach us how to fight once we are prepared.

The main emphasis of these verses is that when a soldier is fighting a spiritual fight, that soldier must be properly equipped for the fight. The Apostle Paul describes this equipment as the "Armor of God'. A soldier's armor is protective equipment that is necessary to minimize or even eliminate injury and death in the event that the enemy connects with his arsenal and weapons. This particular scripture reference identifies this equipment as the "Armor of God'; hence, it is what God has provided for every Christian soldier to use as preparation for Supernatural battles. This 'Armor of God' is what enables Christian soldiers to stand when under attack by *"principalities, powers, rulers of the darkness and spiritual wickedness in high places"*. So great is the emphasis placed on this armor, that the Apostle Paul states that after you've done all that you can do, this Armor will enable you to keep standing! So let's take a closer look at this armor.

Loins girt about with truth – This is essentially a 'belt of truth'. The loins are the area of the mid-section of the body from the upper hips to the lower groin. A belt utilized in this area serves numerous critical purposes. It secures the protective armor worn below it and above it. It also provides a handy location to place any weapon so that the weapon is easily accessible and readily available. It can also be implemented with such width that it provides a layer of protection for the groin area of the soldier. In other words, the belt holds all the other pieces of bodily armor in place. So the Apostle Paul instructs us to put on the belt of truth. To be girded with truth is to be firmly established in the truth of God's Word. God's word is truth.[xvii] This makes the word of God foundational to all the other pieces of spiritual armor. Second, to be girded with truth is to be truthful, genuine and sincere before God and others.

The breastplate of righteousness -- The breastplate is a soldier's protection for his chest and abdominal areas. If a soldier fails to wear a breastplate, an arrow could easily pierce the heart or lungs. This would, in most cases be instant death. The teaching here is that we must protect what's vital to us. Protect what makes us God's children; what places us in the kingdom of God; what makes us acceptable in the eyes of God. As such, the breastplate's critical function is to protect the very thing, our heart, which the enemy attacks. Remember earlier in this book when I explained the soul, I mentioned that in the Bible, the word *'heart'* is used to indicate the soul and spirit miraculously tied together in unison. Therefore, by covering the 'heart', as biblically applied, the breastplate is protecting your soul and spirit. Are not these the things that the enemy desires most to injure, or kill? Proverbs chapter 4 verse 23 states:

"*Keep thy **heart** with all diligence; for out of it are the issues of life.*"

So use the breastplate to protect your soul and spirit from corruption and infiltration by a shrewd wicked enemy.
Paul states that this breastplate should be made of 'righteousness'. In other words, we should be in 'right standing with God. This 'right standing' with God provides protection for our heart (soul and spirit).

Feet shod with the preparation of the gospel of peace -- No soldier can go too far without the proper shoes. Even with all his other weapons, a barefoot soldier would soon become immobilized by the rough terrain taking its toll on his feet. The Apostle Paul describes the shoes necessary for a Christian to successfully war in the spirit as the *"preparation of the gospel of peace"*. The Gospel of peace is to us spiritually, as a good pair of shoes is to a soldier naturally; they provide a firm foundation immediately beneath our feet. No matter how solid the walking surface is, the lack of a good pair of supportive shoes will lead to a catastrophe. When everything else around you is faltering and failing, you can always stand on the Gospel of peace, or the word of God. This should give us confidence in any situation that the God, to whose army we belong, will never allow our enemy to defeat us. Instead, He empowers us to always be victorious.[xix] As long as we have the Gospel of Peace on our feet, we are ensured that we will only walk in the places that are God appointed and God approved. Our shoes will not take us to any other places.

The shield of faith – For this one, the Apostle Paul was very clear. FAITH IS YOUR SHIELD! The soldier's shield was a sizeable metallic shield that required strength and expertise to properly use in battle, thus making it, at times, an offensive weapon. One could beat or bludgeon an enemy into submission, or even death by properly using the shield as an offensive weapon. However, Paul emphasizes that the primary function of this piece of Armor is inherently defensive, stating that the purpose of having this shield is *"wherewith ye shall be able to quench all the fiery darts of the wicked"*. In life, enemies that are not of the world will continually and constantly attack us. These attacks may come in the form of tribulations, trials, sicknesses, natural distresses, social distresses, emotional distresses or financial distresses; there are many avenues that our enemy will use to attack us. (Later in this book, I will introduce and explain the concept of 'Spiritual Sponsors'. I believe God gave me this concept to better enable His children to properly recognize the enemy that has them under attack.) Regardless of the attack, the shield of faith can be used to block, deflect or quench the fiery darts of attack. The word 'fiery' places emphasis on the fervency of the attack. Our supernatural enemies are not playing games. They are committed to their mission to defeat you. (I say they because although we know that the devil is the enemy, he has a hierarchical order of angels and ministers in his army that also do his bidding.[xx] Their intent is to steal, kill or destroy you.[xxi]

Since this piece of equipment is defined as a 'shield of **faith**', let me take a moment and define faith. We often hear faith defined in the context of Hebrews chapter 11 verse 1:

"Now faith is the substance of things hoped for, the evidence of things not seen."

Hebrews 11:1 KJV

This definition is to be applied when believing God for things that cannot be achieved or obtained with the God giving abilities that you possess. It speaks to the confidence in the supernaturally impotent God to accomplish for you what you cannot accomplish alone. (*Understand that it is in God that we live, move and have our being. When I say above 'accomplish alone', I don't mean without God, rather I mean with the God given abilities that you already naturally or physically possess.*)

However, a better and more relevant use of the word **faith** is as reflected in Jude 1 verse 3:

"…ye should earnestly contend for the faith which was once delivered unto the saints."

Jude 1 verse 3 KJV

In Jude, the word faith is used to indicate a complete '**belief system**'. Your Belief System defines what you believe, what governs your actions, what your life expectations are, what character you'll display and ultimately, it governs what actions you will take in critical and distressful situations. Indeed, the proper faith, or '*belief system*', will quench the fiery darts that your enemy launches when you are under attack! This is why the Apostle Paul uses the words "*above all*" when advising that this piece of armor be used. Without the correct 'belief system', there is no way to properly equip yourself with the other pieces of armor and, as you will see later, it becomes impossible to use the weapons provided for battle.

The helmet of salvation – This crucial piece of armor guards the mind! I pray that, after reading and studying the previous section on the soul, you are fully aware of the importance of protecting the mind. We earlier defined the mind as *the presence of the supernatural soul in the natural world*. As such, this is where your spiritual enemies will attack with fervor. Remember how in Romans chapter 7 verse 25, Paul, speaking of life prior to his acceptance of Christ, states:

"So then with the mind, I myself serve the law of God; but with the flesh, the law of sin."

Romans 7:25 KJV

Even the mind of the unsaved seeks to serve God. This is because, as previously explained, the mind is the presence of the soul in the natural world, and the soul comes from God, belongs to God and desires to return to God when your natural life here on earth is completed. So, an attack on the mind of man is an indirect attack on God. When the devil attacks the mind of an unsaved individual, it is an attempt to prevent that individual from acknowledging God, accepting Christ and becoming a member of the kingdom of God. However, when the devil attacks one who has already made the decision to live for God, the purpose is to turn that individual away from Christ and build mistrust of God. Regardless, whether a believer or a non-believer, the purpose is as previously explained; the enemy wants you to be a host for him to re-gain dominion on the earth. You can host by allowing him to influence you, allowing him to control you or allowing him to possess you. Either way, he will use the dominion gained through you for his mission and purpose. So, a helmet to protect the mind is a critical piece of equipment, which if not used, will certainly lead to disaster!

The Apostle Paul instructs us to protect our head, that is or our mind, with salvation. Righteousness protects the afore-mentioned 'heart', but salvation protects the 'mind'. Since the mind is the *presence of the soul in the natural world*, then salvation protects your soul. This protection is the assurance that your soul is saved and will one day it will be reconciled with God, who created it and placed it in you. The only way that your soul can be reconciled with God is if you accept Christ as Lord and Savior! Romans chapter 10, verses 9 and 10 says:

"9. That if thou shalt confess with thy mouth the Lord Jesus, and shalt believe in thine heart that God hath raised him from the dead, thou shalt be saved.
10. For with the heart man believeth unto righteousness; and with the mouth confession is made unto salvation."

Romans 10:9-10 KJV

Without salvation, your soul will be forever separated from God. Ezekiel chapter 18 verse 4 states:

"Behold, all souls are mine; as the soul of the father, so also the soul of the son is mine: the soul that sinneth, it shall die."

Ezekiel 18:4 KJV

If you want to be assured that your soul is protected from eternal death, (*eternal separation from God*), you must wear the Helmet of Salvation and protect your mind! The Helmet of Salvation is necessary to protect the '***presence of the soul in the natural world***'. This means that the helmet of salvation, in protecting your mind, keeps your soul safe, thereby keeping it saved.

The sword of the Spirit – Of all of the equipment that the Apostle Paul advises us to use, this is the only piece designed, created and primarily used as an offensive

74

weapon. The sword is used to attack and counter-attack an enemy until the it seriously wounds or kills the assailant. The counsel of the Apostle Paul is that the weapon for defeating supernatural enemies is "THE WORD OF GOD." This is an 'effective and efficient weapon' that has proved to be deadly to spiritual enemies. When understood and applied correctly, this weapon hits its target with precision and simply annihilates it. Hebrews chapter 4 verse 12 says:

"For the word of God is quick, and powerful, and sharper than any twoedged sword, piercing even to the dividing asunder of soul and spirit, and of the joints and marrow, and is a discerner of the thoughts and intents of the heart."

Hebrews 4:12 KJV

This is truly an effective weapon when used properly. This weapon is so effective because when you use it, you are in effect allowing God to do the fighting. That's because the Word of God is God! John chapter 1 verse 1 states:

"In the beginning was the Word, and the Word was with God, and the Word was God."

John 1:1 KJV

So when you use the Sword of the Spirit (***Word of God***) against supernatural enemies, you are effectively using the omnipotent **God** against those enemies, **and the omnipotent God will always defeat supernatural enemies**! However, you cannot use the Word of God unless you learn, know and understand it. This is why the Bibles instructs in Second Timothy chapter 2 verse 15:

"Study to shew thyself approved unto God, a workman that needeth not to be ashamed, rightly dividing the word of truth."

2 Timothy 2:15 KJV

Your success or failure in using the Sword of the Spirit rests solely on the correct knowledge, understanding and proper application of God's word. This places extra importance on Bible Class and Sunday School in the local church. The Word of God is not a singular weapon, but each verse can be applied with surgical precision when striking back at the supernatural enemies that oppose you. You are assured victory when this Word is properly used. I will provide greater detail later, at step four, as I explain the usage of our available weapons. This is only step one of the four-step process for successfully waging war against supernatural opposition.

Praying always with all prayer and supplication in the Spirit – This may possibly be the most crucial piece of equipment on which the Apostle Paul provides instruction. With all of the armor that we are instructed to put on, it is only effective if we pray. The instruction to be always praying is the same advice given in Luke chapter 18 verse 1:

"And he spake a parable unto them to this end, that men ought always to pray, and not to faint;"

Luke 18:1 KJV

The same advice is given in First Thessalonians chapter 5 verse 17:

"Pray without ceasing."

1 Thessalonians 5:17 KJV

So the advice and guidance here is to have a consistent and continual prayer life, because prayer is the tool that enables us to realize victory in the supernatural world. **Important to note, this tool only enables victory if you use it (pray) consistently and continually.** Consistent and continual prayer strengthens the soul, and combined with fasting it subdues the **flesh**. As such, it makes your soul the **dominant you,** which provides the foundation for the function of prayer in spiritual warfare. Later, when I explain how to access the battlefield, I will explain the specific role that prayer plays when fighting a spiritual battle.

Let me reiterate this point because of its importance. Earlier in this book, I repeatedly talked about making your soul the 'dominant' you in this world. Prayer, when done with fasting, is the tool that does this. Consistent and continual prayer with fasting strengthens the soul while simultaneously subduing the flesh (body). When prayer and fasting are consistently utilized together in a person with a regenerated spirit, (*a saved person*), they work to bring the flesh into subjection, thereby allowing the soul to be dominant. The Apostle Paul says in First Corinthians chapter 9 verse 27:

"But I keep under my body, and bring it into subjection:"
1 Corinthians 9:27 KJV

Once the flesh is subdued and the soul is dominant, you are then ready to access the battlefield where your spiritual enemies reside. Getting to that battlefield is also a function of prayer. I will cover that in step three, "Getting to the Battlefield".

Watching thereunto with all perseverance and supplication for all saints – Watching should always accompany prayer. In Matthew chapter 26 verse 41, Jesus advises his disciples in the Garden of Gethsemane:

"Watch and pray, that ye enter not into temptation:"
Matthew 26:41 KJV

Be alert and keep an eye out for the wicked devices employed by Satan. In Second Corinthians chapter 2 verse 11, the Apostle Paul writes:

"Lest Satan should get an advantage of us: for we are not ignorant of his devices."
2 Corinthians 2:11 KJV

We watch while we pray because we are not ignorant of Satan's devices and we don't want him to gain an advantage simply because we are not alert!

Your watching should be done with perseverance and supplication. We must be committed to protecting ourselves from the enemy at all costs. Not every attack begins with a violent action. Some attacks begin disguised as favorable actions that appear to support your position. However, the enemy's strategy is always focused on the end goal, so you have to be careful not to overlook clandestine actions that lead to a weakening of your defenses. Overlooking these actions will place you in a compromised and indefensible position when the truth of the attack is unveiled. Perseverance is watching and waiting while using discernment to determine which actions originated with your enemy and which actions are harmless and can be ignored or overlooked. A mistake in properly assessing these actions can lead to your defeat. Moreover, be earnest while praying. Acknowledge your limitations when you are making requests of the omnipotent God. Humble yourself before God and remain humble while making requests. James chapter 4 verse 10 says:

"Humble yourselves in the sight of the Lord, and he shall lift you up."

James 4:10 KJV

And as I close this step, I close with the words of the Apostle Paul in verse 18, **"for all saints"**. The prayers with perseverance and supplication should be made for **all saints**, not just you only. The emphasis here is on *'all saints'* and not *'everybody'*. The reason this is emphasized is that an army is a unit made up of multiple individual soldiers. Each soldier brings their unique abilities to the army, but the success in the overall battle depends on each individual soldier working together with other soldiers to defeat the army of the enemy. In other words, you are not in this fight alone, and there are other saints in this same army fighting the same enemy army as you. We should be fighting together to defeat this enemy. We should be united by the commonality of our faith (belief system) and the shared enemy that opposes everything that God has established!

If we can accomplish the things commanded us in Ephesians chapter 6 verses 13 -18, we will be well **prepared** to engage, fight and defeat opposition from the Supernatural World!

Step Two – Identify the Enemy That Opposes You

At first glance, this appears to be a very easy step. You can't have a fight without opposing forces. We have already taken considerable time and effort to show why we have an enemy, as well as the goals, mission and purpose of this enemy. So on the surface, it appears that all that remains is for us to name this enemy. However, it really is a bit more detailed than that. We can begin by identifying the commander of the opposing forces. In First Peter chapter 5 verse 8, it says:

"Be sober, be vigilant; because your adversary the devil, as a roaring lion, walketh about, seeking whom he may devour:"

1 Peter 5:8 KJV

This verse leaves no question as to who our enemy is. This enemy is not a single enemy. He is not fighting alone. In Second Corinthians chapter 11 verses 14-15, we are warned:

"14. And no marvel; for Satan himself is transformed into an angel of light.
15. Therefore it is no great thing if his ministers also be transformed as the ministers of righteousness; whose end shall be according to their works."

2 Corinthians 11:14-15 KJV

So Satan has angels[xxii] and ministers under his control that have transformed themselves into 'ministers of righteousness' for this fight. He actually has a legitimate army working on his behalf in an attempt to bring him victory, but how does this army create so much chaos, cause so much pain, and raise so much hell? By not being easily recognized as the ministers of Satan. They function undercover. They attack, disguised as ministers of righteousness. Remember we stated earlier that not all attacks of the enemy begin violently. Many times, these attacks are disguised as processes of nature, or things that seem to work in your favor, when in reality; it is Satan or one of his ministers systematically leading you into a trap. I will now introduce you to the term '**Spiritual Sponsor**'.

I believe that God gave me this term to equip His people to be more efficient, and thereby more effective, when fighting personal supernatural attacks. A **Spiritual Sponsor** is a powerful supernatural force that works in the background, initiating, supporting and sponsoring an attack that occurs on the surface. It is not what you see as the attack, but rather, it provides the support and energy that the attack needs to be successful. The **Spiritual Sponsor** manifests itself as a surface attack to direct your attention away from the true source of the attack, and get you to focus on the surface appearance, rather than the true root of the problem.

For example, you may think that the problems you are encountering on your job are because your co-workers have

82

issues with you, but in actuality, it's Satan or one of these ministers initiating and supporting an attack through the co-workers. If they can get you to focus your energy and your strategy on the co-workers, they can continue their attack on you without challenge. **Spiritual Sponsors** succeed by getting you to focus on the resultant pain instead of the root, or source of the pain. If they succeed in re-directing your attention away from them, you will most certainly be defeated because of your failure to identify and recognize the real enemy. This is why the Apostle Paul stressed that we are not fighting against "flesh and blood". [xxiii] Too many times, we fail to recognize the real source of our opposition and waste energy and time fighting the appearance of an enemy, while the **Spiritual Sponsor** for the opposition to us goes unchecked. This is true with many diseases, sicknesses, financial distresses, social stresses, etc. This is why earlier, I stated that perseverance is watching and waiting while using **discernment**. The enemy specializes in clandestine operations, and if he can attack unnoticed or undetected, he will, at the very least, cause serious damage. The enemy operating in this 'undercover' manner poses grave danger and the longer he goes undetected, the greater his chances of defeating you become. Discerning of spirits is a necessity when warring against supernatural spiritual enemies.

We find this verse in Acts chapter 19 verses 11 and 12:

"*11. And God wrought special miracles by the hands of Paul:*

12. So that from his body were brought unto the sick handkerchiefs or aprons, and the diseases departed from them, and the evil spirits went out of them."

Acts 19:11-12 KJV

When Paul was preaching, he anointed handkerchiefs and aprons. These articles (handkerchiefs and aprons) were then sent to the sick. Nevertheless, look at what happened when these articles reached the sick. ***"The diseases departed from them and the evil spirits went out of them"***. This is a clear indication that the diseases really weren't the root of the problem, but rather the problem was initiated, empowered and supported by the evil spirits working in the background. So instead of praying for healing of the disease, Paul discerned that the root was Spiritual Sponsors, so he addressed these Spiritual Sponsors by sending anointed aprons and handkerchief that drove out the evil spirits, thus terminating the sickness and disease. I am not saying that all sicknesses and diseases have Spiritual Sponsors; some come within the natural process of life. However, when affliction does set in, promptly identifying and addressing the root of the affliction can be the difference between life and death. Acts chapter 10 verse 38 reads:

"How God anointed Jesus of Nazareth with the Holy Ghost and with power: who went about doing good, and healing all that were oppressed of the devil; for God was with him."

Acts 10:38 KJV

It makes clear that Jesus **healed** those that were oppressed by the devil. So whereas some sicknesses and disease come within the natural processes of living and life, many have **Spiritual Sponsors**, and healing is dependent on identifying, engaging and defeating the **Spiritual Sponsor** for that illness.

In Matthew chapter 6 verse 23, Jesus provides the example for dealing with **Spiritual Sponsors**.

"But he turned, and said unto Peter, Get thee behind me, Satan: thou art an offence unto me: for thou savourest not the things that be of God, but those that be of men."
Matthew 6:23 KJV

Here, Jesus looks at Peter, but He specifically addresses and rebukes Satan. Why? Because Jesus discerned that Satan was the **Spiritual Sponsor** for Peter's actions. So if Jesus wanted the action to cease, He had to stop it at its root. He had to look beyond the surface action and defeat the **Spiritual Sponsor** working in the background.

So, the proper identification of the enemy is crucial to realizing victory. As you will see in the step explaining the usage of your weapons, proper identification of your enemies leads to the utilization of the proper weapon against them. This greatly increases your chances of being victorious.

Step Three – Access the Battlefield to Engage Your Enemy

So you've prepared yourself and you've identified your enemy. The very next step is to engage this enemy on the battlefield. I'll make this plain and simple; you can't fight without engaging the enemy. This is where the constitution of man is extremely important. Satan, his angels and his ministers are all residents of the Supernatural or Spiritual World. In order to confront them, we must enter into the world where they reside and engage them there.

At first, it would appear that we are at a disadvantage, but let's recall the constitution of man. God created man with three parts: a body, soul and spirit. If you remember, I emphasized earlier that your body is you in the Natural World, whereas your soul is you in the Supernatural or Spiritual World. This dual citizenship means that your soul already resides in the world where your spiritual enemies live; you just need to confront, engage, fight and defeat them.

Since your soul is you in that supernatural world, then your soul must do the fighting for you there. Remember that the Spirit animates (brings to life) both the natural body and the supernatural soul. The body comes to life in the Natural World, whereas the soul comes to life in the Supernatural World. *I hope that by now you realize why so much emphasis was placed on making the soul the dominant you.* Also, remember that I showed that consistent and continual prayer is the tool that makes your soul the dominant you. Equally important emphasis was placed on the need to have a regenerated spirit when engaging in war with spiritual beings. It is dangerous, personally destructive and outright risky to reside in the Supernatural World, as your soul does, without a regenerated spirit, equipped with all of the benefits, strengths and protection. Yet, millions of people who have not accepted Christ, or have flat out rejected Christ take this risk daily. THANK GOD FOR THE INHERENT RESISTANCE TO SATAN THAT WE HAVE BECAUSE OF OUR CONSTITUTION!

Natural man has been given dominion over all that exists in the natural realm. He only reports up to a sovereign God! However, the power structure is quite different in the Supernatural World. In the Supernatural World, of course, God is still the omnipotent almighty sovereign ruler, but there are angels that are of higher order than the **regenerated** spirit man; there is the evil spirit Satan, who is of higher order than the **un-regenerated** spirit man. There are evil principalities and powers that are of higher order than the **un-regenerated** spirit man.

Spirit man must be regenerated if he is to be empowered to successfully live in and wage war against the enemies in the spirit realm!

When I use the term 'spirit man' here, I am referring to the part of tri-parte man that lives in the Supernatural or Spiritual World. This is the **soul**! And when I say regenerated spirit

87

man, I am speaking of a soul that is being driven by a regenerated spirit, as explained earlier. This means, by contrast, that the un-regenerated spirit man is a soul that is being driven by a spirit that has not been regenerated. To make it simple, you could say:

Regenerated spirit man is a saved soul
Un-regenerated spirit man is an unsaved soul

With our dual citizenship, we inherently live in both the natural and supernatural worlds. Natural man can't access the Supernatural World, but your soul is already there. So getting to the spiritual battlefield is really you becoming aware of your soul's actions and activities in the Supernatural World.

THE ONLY WAY EVER SPELLED OUT IN THE BIBLE TO BECOME AWARE OF YOUR SOUL'S ACTIVIES IN THE SPIRITUAL WORLD IS THROUGH _PRAYER_!

If you've grown up in church or been around church-going people, you've probably been told what prayer is and that it does many things:

1. Prayer makes us aware of His presence
2. Prayer helps us see and hear His voice
3. Prayer changes us
4. Prayer changes the atmosphere
5. Prayer gives us hope

6. Prayer brings light to the darkness in our hearts
7. Prayer helps us tear down walls
8. Prayer helps us become who He has called us to be
9. Prayer helps us to be more selfless
10. Prayer makes us more like Him

However, in the context of spiritual warfare, prayer makes you spiritually aware of your soul's activities, thereby placing you on the spiritual battlefield to confront your enemy. It is as if prayer is your transportation vehicle that carries you from the Natural World into the Spiritual World during spiritual wartime.

Let's consider and examine a few biblical examples of prayer making individuals aware of their soul's activities in the supernatural world.

Acts chapter 10 verses 9 - 16 reads:

9. On the morrow, as they went on their journey, and drew nigh unto the city, Peter went up upon the housetop to pray about the sixth hour:
10. And he became very hungry, and would have eaten: but while they made ready, he fell into a trance,
11. And saw heaven opened, and a certain vessel descending unto him, as it had been a great sheet knit at the four corners, and let down to the earth:

12. Wherein were all manner of fourfooted beasts of the earth, and wild beasts, and creeping things, and fowls of the air.

13. And there came a voice to him, Rise, Peter; kill, and eat.

14. But Peter said, Not so, Lord; for I have never eaten any thing that is common or unclean.

15. And the voice spake unto him again the second time, What God hath cleansed, that call not thou common.

16. This was done thrice: and the vessel was received up again into heaven.

Acts 10:9-16 KJV

When Peter prayed, he fell into a trance! This is evidence that his prayer placed him in a state where he became more aware of his soul's activities in the Supernatural or Spiritual World. Once the vision began, Peter was, at that time and during this event, aware of his soul's activities, in the Supernatural or Spirit World because he saw things that were not physical, material or natural. How did he become aware of his soul's activities in the Spirit World? This all began with his prayer, so it is obvious that his prayer did this for him. It got him to the spiritual battlefield! Peter was not fighting a Spiritual War in this instance, but his prayer placed him in the world where spiritual enemies live. So if he needed to fight, all he would have to do is use his weapons.

Even if we analyze Cornelius in this same chapter, we find that his prayers also made him aware of his soul's action in the Spirit World. [xxiv] His prayers also got him to the spiritual battlefield!

Let's look at the example of Paul in Acts chapter 27 verses 21 - 24:

21. But after long abstinence Paul stood forth in the midst of them, and said, Sirs, ye should have hearkened unto me, and not have loosed from Crete, and to have gained this harm and loss.
22. And now I exhort you to be of good cheer: for there shall be no loss of any man's life among you, but of the ship.
23. For there stood by me this night the angel of God, whose I am, and whom I serve,
24. Saying, Fear not, Paul; thou must be brought before Caesar: and, lo, God hath given thee all them that sail with thee.

Acts 27:21-24 KJV

In the midst of being tossed and turned in the sea, Paul disappears for prayer. While in prayer, an angel visits Paul and gives him instructions. ANGELS ARE SPIRIT BEINGS THAT RESIDE IN THE SUPERNATURAL, OR SPIRITUAL WORLD! Paul's prayer would have had to make him aware of his soul's activities in the Spiritual World for him to see these spiritual beings that live in the Spiritual World.

We can even go back to the Old Testament and look at Elijah. First Kings chapter 19 verses 4 and 5 reads:

4. But he himself went a day's journey into the wilderness, and came and sat down under a juniper tree: and he requested for himself that he might die; and said, It is enough; now, O Lord, take away my life; for I am not better than my fathers.
5. And as he lay and slept under a juniper tree, behold, then an angel touched him, and said unto him, Arise and eat.

1 Kings 19:4 KJV

I like this one because it verifies that the process of becoming aware of your soul's activities in the Spiritual World existed even under the law. This would be expected because man received a soul, and therewith, dual citizenship at creation.

Elijah prayed himself to sleep, but his prayer made him aware of his soul's activities in the Spiritual World. So, when he fell asleep, he became unconscious and unaware of the natural world because of sleep, but he was fully conscious spiritually and aware of his soul's activities in the Spiritual World. That's when the angel, a being that lives in the Spiritual World, visits him and gives him instructions.

I could go on with biblical examples where when men prayed, they became aware of their soul's activities in the Spiritual World. The Bible record the spiritual events or occurrences that took place whenever this occurred. Need I mention Jesus at the Mount of Transfiguration, or Jesus praying in the Garden of Gethsemane? In both of these instances, the man Jesus prayed; in one instance spiritual beings (angels) appeared and in the other instance the transfiguration, a spiritual occurrence took place.

So getting to the battlefield is really praying yourself into a state where you become aware of your soul's activities in the Spiritual World. When this happens, you will see, hear and interact with spiritual beings. Your enemies, Satan and his minions, reside in this world; so if you are going to confront them, you must fervently pray to get there.

Let me emphasize that the prayer for getting to the battlefield is in addition to the consistent and continual prayer life that's required to make your soul the dominant you. This prayer is made when fighting a spiritual war. It is made on the foundation of a consistent and continual prayer life. The purpose of this prayer in the strategy of spiritual warfare, as the examples have shown, is to place you in the world where your spiritual enemy resides.

We have ample biblical basis and foundation to support the fact that in the context of spiritual warfare, prayer is not your weapon, but rather, prayer is more like a transport vehicle that places you in a state where you become aware of your soul's activities within the Spiritual World. It is in this Supernatural or Spiritual World where your spiritual enemies live; hence, it is the only place that can be used as a spiritual battlefield.

You cannot succeed in spiritual warfare without using prayer to get to the battlefield. You can quote as many scriptures as you can remember. However, if you have no consistent and continual prayer life to make your soul the dominant you, then use prayer on top of that to become aware of your soul's activities in the Spiritual World, then you are only beating the air with your scriptures because you have failed to enter the world where your enemies live. In First Corinthians chapter 9 verse 26, Paul writes:

"So fight I, not as one that beateth the air:"
1 Corinthians 9:26 KJV

So basically, and in the most plain language,
"YOU MUST PRAY YOUR WAY ONTO THE BATTLEFIELD!

If you fight on a foundation of prayer, then your prayer will place you in the Spiritual World where you can confront, engage and defeat Satan and his minions. Without prayer, you will never get to that world, so when you begin to fight, you are merely beating the air. This is the reason Jesus, the Apostles and the Bible all emphasize the necessity of PRAYER for the believer. Without a consistent and continuous prayer life, the believer is destined to be defeated

94

time and time again when confronted by a supernatural or spiritual enemy.

I have now defined and explained the role of prayer both in making your soul the dominant you and within the context of spiritual warfare; now let me make another point that is foundational in understanding this step before I move on to the weapons we have to fight with.

YOU DO NOT FIGHT SPIRITUAL WARFARE <u>WITH</u> PRAYER!

YOU FIGHT SPIRITUAL WARFARE <u>IN</u> PRAYER!

Step Four – Use the Weapons That God Has Provided for Fighting Supernatural Enemies

Now that you've:

1. Prepared Yourself for Spiritual Battle
2. Identified Your Enemy
3. Prayed Your Way onto The Battlefield

The only thing remaining is to select a weapon and fight. In all the preparation for war in the Supernatural World, the Bible only provides for us one group of weapons.

The Word of God!

"The *sword of the Spirit, which is the word of God*:"
Ephesians 6:17 KJV

The Word of God has many functions and performs many duties, but in the context of Spiritual Warfare, it is as The Apostle Paul says, '*The Sword of The Spirit*'!

When our '*Regenerated Spirit Driven Soul*' is engaging in warfare in the *Supernatural or Spiritual World*, what better weapon to have than the '**Sword of The Spirit**'. The name itself (*Sword of The Spirit*) indicates that this weapon was designed and created for such a task as defeating our spiritual enemies.

Such a formidable and powerful weapon we have when we possess knowledge and understanding of God's word. The writer of Hebrews lauds this weapon for its might, power and precision! Hebrews chapter 4 verse 12 reads:

"For the word of God is quick, and powerful, and sharper than any twoedged sword, piercing even to the dividing asunder of soul and spirit, and of the joints and marrow, and is a discerner of the thoughts and intents of the heart."
Hebrews 4:12 KJV

The word of God always makes us victorious because it always performs the actions for which it was purposed. Simply put, **IT NEVER FAILS!** Isaiah chapter 55 verses 10-11 reads:

"10. For as the rain cometh down, and the snow from heaven, and returneth not thither, but watereth the earth, and maketh it bring forth and bud, that it may give seed to the sower, and bread to the eater:
11. So shall my word be that goeth forth out of my mouth: it shall not return unto me void, but it shall accomplish that which I please, and it shall prosper in the thing whereto I sent it."
Isaiah 55:10-11 KJV

YOU ARE GUARANTEED TO NEVER LOSE A SPIRITUAL BATTLE IF YOUR WEAPON IS THE WORD OF GOD!

The real reason that success is guaranteed when warring in the spirit <u>the right way</u>, with the word of God as a weapon, is that when you are fighting with the Word of God, God is actually doing the fighting because the ***Word of God is God***! John chapter 1 verse 14 reads:

"And the Word was made flesh, and dwelt among us, (and we beheld his glory, the glory as of the only begotten of the Father,) full of grace and truth."

John 1:14 KJV

Consider Second Corinthians chapter 10 verse 4:

"For the weapons of our warfare are not carnal, but mighty through God to the pulling down of strong holds;"

2 Corinthians 10:4 KJV

You should take note that in Second Corinthians chapter 10 verse 4, the word ***weapons*** is plural. The Bible is not a single weapon, but each verse is a weapon, to be used with precision to obtain victory against our enemy with specificity! This emphasizes the need for Bible knowledge and understanding.

Each verse of God's word is quick, powerful and sharper than any double-edged sword!

So you should use the weapon that is most appropriate and effective for the battle that you are fighting.

If your current enemy is sickness, you need to learn, remember and understand the verses of scripture for healing! *These are your weapons!* **Use Them!**

If your current enemy is poverty, you need to learn, remember and understand the verses of scripture for wealth! *These are your weapons! Use Them!*

If your current enemy is depression or sadness, you need to learn, remember and understand the verses of scripture for happiness and joy! *These are your weapons!* **Use Them!**

If your current enemy is need, you need to learn, remember and understand the verses of scripture for God's provision! *These are your weapons!* **Use Them!**

Whatever it is that you are fighting, you need to learn, remember and understand the verses pertinent to that opposition because **the scriptures that you know and use are the weapons that you fight with**!

This is the very reason that we are instructed in scripture to study the scriptures, search the scriptures and understand the scriptures.

Bible study is like military basic training for Spiritual Warfare![xxv]

So there you have it! If Spiritual Warfare is fought utilizing the God inspired method of this book, you are guaranteed to always be victorious. Second Corinthians chapter 2 verse 14 affirms this victory:

"Now thanks be unto God, which always causeth us to triumph in Christ,"

2 Corinthians 2:14 KJV

And so does First Corinthians chapter 15 verse 57:

"But thanks be to God, which giveth us the victory through our Lord Jesus Christ."

1 Corinthians 15:57 KJV

In summary, the following method guarantees victory over any and all spiritual enemies:

1. *Prepare for spiritual warfare (Allow God to regenerate your spirit and put on the Armor of God)*
2. *Identify and understand your enemy (Be specific in identifying your enemy because you will need to use the correct weapon against him)*
3. *Use prayer to transition you onto the spiritual battlefield (Consistent and continual prayer makes the regenerated spirit driven soul dominant; specific fervent prayer while sighting spiritual battles makes*

you aware of your soul's activities in the Spiritual World)

4. *Once prayer puts you on the spiritual battlefield, use scripture as your weapon against your enemy. (Specific opposition requires specific specialized scripture or weapons)*

I have now provided you with the **biblical best practice** for **'Winning Spiritual Wars'**, destroying spiritual yokes and pulling down spiritual strongholds. This method is tested, tried and true! Men and women throughout the Bible have employed it with tremendous success.

I will conclude this book by analyzing the example that Jesus provided us for spiritual warfare.

You will see that the four-step method explained and spelled out in this book follows Jesus' example to the letter, *Line by Line, Precept by Precept*!

5

The Example of Jesus

¹ Then was Jesus led up of the Spirit into the wilderness to be tempted of the devil.
² And when he had fasted forty days and forty nights, he was afterward an hungred.
³ And when the tempter came to him, he said, "If thou be the Son of God, command that these stones be made bread."
⁴ But he answered and said, "It is written, Man shall not live by bread alone, but by every word that proceedeth out of the mouth of God."
⁵ Then the devil taketh him up into the holy city, and setteth him on a pinnacle of the temple,
⁶ And saith unto him, "If thou be the Son of God, cast thyself down: for it is written, He shall give his angels

charge concerning thee: and in their hands they shall bear thee up, lest at any time thou dash thy foot against a stone."

⁷ Jesus said unto him, "It is written again, Thou shalt not tempt the Lord thy God."

⁸ Again, the devil taketh him up into an exceeding high mountain, and sheweth him all the kingdoms of the world, and the glory of them

⁹ And saith unto him, "All these things will I give thee, if thou wilt fall down and worship me."

¹⁰ Then saith Jesus unto him, "Get thee hence, Satan: for it is written, Thou shalt worship the Lord thy God, and him only shalt thou serve."

¹¹ Then the devil leaveth him, and, behold, angels came and ministered unto him.

Matthew 4: 9-11 KJV

Step 1 -- Jesus Prepared Himself

Jesus spirit had been re-generated so He had a regenerated spirit animating, quickening or driving both his body and soul. Luke chapter 3 verses 21 and 22 reads:

"21. Now when all the people were baptized, it came to pass, that Jesus also being baptized, and praying, the heaven was opened,

22. And the Holy Ghost descended in a bodily shape like a dove upon him, and a voice came from heaven, which said, Thou art my beloved Son; in thee I am well pleased.”

Luke 3:21-22 KJV

Step 2 -- Jesus Identified His Enemy

Jesus knew His enemy as identified in John chapter 14 verse 30. He said that He had nothing to do with, or no common ground, this enemy.

"Hereafter I will not talk much with you: for the prince of this world cometh, and hath nothing in me.”

John 14:30 KJV

Step 3 -- Jesus prayed (and fasted) his way onto the battlefield to confront His enemy there

Our record of the life of Jesus shows that the man, Jesus, (The Son of Man), had a consistent and continual prayer life that included fasting. This made His soul dominant. So when confronted by His enemy Satan, He fervently prayed to become aware of His soul's activities in the Spiritual World.

Matthew chapter 4 verse 1 and 2 reads:

"1. Then was Jesus led up of the Spirit into the wilderness to be tempted of the devil.
2. And when he had fasted forty days and forty nights, he was afterward and hungred.”

Matthew 4:1 KJV

Step 4 – Once on the battlefield, Jesus used the Word of God as weapons of precision.

For each attack of Satan, Jesus fought back with the '**Sword of The Spirit**'. Note the specificity of the scriptures He used matched the specific attack of Satan.

Matthew chapter 4 verses 4, 7 and 10 reads:

"*4. But he answered and said, "It is written, Man shall not live by bread alone, but by every word that proceedeth out of the mouth of God."*

Deuteronomy 8:3 KJV

"*7. Jesus said unto him, It is written again, Thou shalt not tempt the Lord thy God."*

Deuteronomy 6:16 KJV

"*10. Then saith Jesus unto him, Get thee hence, Satan: for it is written, Thou shalt worship the Lord thy God, and him only shalt thou serve."*

Deuteronomy 6:13 KJV

So as you can see, Jesus clearly employed the method put forth in this book and it resulted in victory over His enemy.

You too can experience victory by following the example of Jesus, because this example was recorded in the Bible to be our '*Best Practice*' for **Warring in The Spirit**!

APPENDIX

Terms as used in this book

Regenerated Spirit – A completely new spirit. The spirit of man that is renewed upon acceptance of Jesus Christ as Lord and Savior.

Un-regenerated Spirit – The spirit of man prior to acceptance of Christ as Lord and Savior. This is the spirit that all men have at conception.

Regenerated Spirit Driven Soul – The soul after one accepts Christ as Lord and Savior; a saved soul; the soul of a Christian, believer or a saved person.

Un-regenerated Spirit Driven Soul – The soul prior to accepting Christ as Lord and Savior; the soul of an unbeliever (unsaved or unrepentant person).

Dominant Soul – The soul of a believer that has, through prayer, fasting and study of the word, become equally as strong or stronger than the flesh. The person with a dominant soul leading in this material world will make Godly choices and, because of those choices, will experience miracles and supernatural occurrences because the soul of man is supernatural and not limited to the natural limitations of the physical world.

Realm – region, sphere or world

Supernatural World – The spirit world or realm where the soul of man resides; this term is used synonymously with *Spiritual World*.

Spiritual World – see Supernatural World above.

Spirit Realm – see Supernatural World above.

Natural Realm – The natural material physical world that we physically live in.

Spiritual Sponsor – A supernatural spiritual force operating in the background disguising itself as any of the many problems that manifest as sickness, distresses, poverty, etc., in the natural physical world.

Best Practice – The process or procedure that is biblically supported and accepted to be correct and is the most effective.

**You can bring a '*Warring in The Spirit*'
Conference/Seminar to your local church or group.**

This book was birthed out of the one-day '**Warring in The
Spirit**' conference conducted by Pastor Henry L. Razor.

Pastor Razor is available to deliver this conference to your
local church, worship assembly or community group.

For more information or to schedule a conference, contact
The Faith Place Bible Institute at:

Contact Us - http://www.henryrazorministries.net
Email - henryrazorministries@gmail.com

Telephone: (773) 255 -9773

Henry Razor Sr. Pastor
Faith Hope & Charity Ministries
354 W 71st Street, Chicago, Il 60621
Streaming Live Each Sunday Morning at 10:00 AM on
Facebook @ Faith Place-Chicago and YouTube @ FHC TV

When is The Soul Created?

How are human souls created?[xxvi]

This explanation of the origin of the human soul is taken from 'Compelling Truth'. The link to this article on their site is in the appendix of this book and is referenced in the heading of this section.

The Bible does not tell us exactly how human souls are created, but we can speculate about the process based on what the Bible does say. From the biblical record, people have extrapolated two possible ways that human souls are created. These two views are called Traducianism and Creationism. There is also a third view, which lacks biblical support.

Traducianism is the idea that a person's soul is created at the same time their physical body is created—that is, the soul is generated from the physical parents just as is the physical body of a child. This theory is plausible because the Bible says that God made Adam a "living soul" when He breathed life into him (Genesis 2:7 KJV), but this action is not recorded elsewhere in the Bible, implying that all human beings came by their souls in another way. Since Adam was the father of all men and women, physically speaking, and we know we inherit our sin nature from Adam as well (Romans 5:12), it is plausible to assume that the soul is also inherited. Traducianism depends on the assumption that the body and soul are intertwined, and that in a sense, the soul depends upon the body for existence, and the method of generation of the soul by a physical process is unclear. This is a weakness in the theory.

The **Creationist** viewpoint says that God creates a soul each time a human being is conceived. The Bible seems to place a separation between the creation of the physical body and the creation of the soul (Ecclesiastes 12:7; Isaiah 42:5; Zechariah 12:1; Hebrews 12:9). There are two problems with this theory. One, Genesis 2:2–3 can be interpreted that once God was done creating everything during the first six days, He ceased to create anything new. Second, since all human beings are subject to the sin nature, which came from Adam, how does the soul become poisoned by sin? Is it a result of being in the body? We simply cannot answer these questions without information that God has chosen not to reveal at this time.

A third theory, often held by new age religions and faiths that depend upon a reincarnation view of the soul, is that a "warehouse" of souls exists in heaven, all of which were created by God at the beginning; and each time a new body is created, God attaches a soul to it. This view has no biblical support whatsoever.

Whether Traducianism, Creationism or some other yet-to-be-realized truth holds the answer to the generation of human souls, we know that all souls originate with God, who is the Maker of all things that exist (John 1:1–3).

[i] 2 Kings 6:8-17

[ii] 1 Peter 5:8

[iii] Revelation 12:9

[iv]
https://www.blueletterBible.org/faq/don_stewart/don_stewart_654.cfm

[v] Genesis 1:31
[vi] Google Dictionary
[vii] St Luke 10:18

[viii] 1 Corinthians 15:47
[ix] Genesis 2:7

[x] Genesis 1:28
[xi] Ecclesiastes 12:7
[xii] 1 Corinthians 11:14
[xiii] St John 6:63
[xiv] St. Luke 14:31-32
[xv] Ezekiel 28:14
[xvi] Revelation 20:10
[xvii] St John 17:17
[xviii] 1 Peter 2:12
[xix] 1 Corinthians 15:57
[xx] 2 Corinthians 11:14-15
[xxi] St John 10:10
[xxii] Revelation 12:7-9
[xxiii] Ephesians 6:12
[xxiv] Acts 10:9-16
[xxv] 2 Timothy 2:15; John 5:39; Proverbs 4:7
[xxvi] https://www.compellingtruth.org/souls-created.html

CPSIA information can be obtained
at www.ICGtesting.com
Printed in the USA
BVHW021954130521
607264BV00008B/232